THE TRANSCENDENTAL PROFESSIONAL

Cultivating Elite and Enlightened Professional Transformation

Premji Boominathan

Contents

Author Biography

Premji Boominathan, an avant-garde luminary with a quarter-century of traversing the professional realm, dons many hats with finesse – Agile Maestro, Strategist, Product Management Sage, and a Transformation Virtuoso. His profound belief centers on nature as the repository of solutions for contemporary and impending global predicaments. For 26 years, Premji has artfully harnessed nature's principles and sagacity to unravel challenges, not only for himself but as a beacon for others. Additionally, he is a certified Independent Director, Environmental, Social and Governance (ESG) expert, and a certified Digital Director.

In the intricate tapestry of his professional journey, Premji Boominathan stands as a seasoned guide, weaving through the intricate corridors of Agile methodology. A trailblazing Agile Coach, his expertise extends to the nuanced realm of Scaled Agile practices, where he orchestrates a symphony of methodologies to harmonize the discordant notes of complexity.

As a Strategic Maestro, Premji navigates the strategic landscape with a finesse that borders on artistry. His canvas is dotted with strokes of innovation, where each strategic move is not a mere decision but a calculated dance with uncertainty. With 25 years of insights, he metamorphoses problems into opportunities, shaping destinies with each strategic stroke.

Venturing into the labyrinth of Product Management, Premji assumes the role of a sage, distilling wisdom from years of traversing the landscape of innovation. His consultancy extends beyond conventional boundaries, crafting a narrative where products are not just commodities but living entities shaped by a profound understanding of market dynamics and user needs.

Transformation, in the hands of Premji, transcends the mundane and becomes a transformative journey akin to nature's perpetual renewal. His coaching prowess extends beyond the surface, delving into the core of organizational metamorphosis. Premji's transformative touch is not just about change; it's about orchestrating a symphony where every note resonates with the essence of growth and evolution.

Nature, for Premji Boominathan, isn't just a source of inspiration; it's a treasure trove of solutions waiting to be unearthed. His philosophy intertwines with nature's wisdom, advocating for a profound understanding of natural principles. This understanding, according to Premji, is a key to unlocking solutions not only for today's challenges but for those that loom on the horizon.

In a world inundated with conventional approaches, Premji Boominathan is a transcendental force, propelling individuals and organizations towards holistic growth. His journey isn't just a testament to experience but a saga of leveraging nature's brilliance to illuminate the path of innovation, strategy, and transformation. With each stride, Premji leaves an indelible mark, an imprint that echoes the profound resonance of a professional journey sculpted by nature's timeless wisdom.

Premji Boominathan, the visionary mind behind "The Transcendental Framework: Advancing along the 7G Trail," unveils a profound journey interwoven with the wisdom of the 7 chakras, guiding individuals towards a holistic elevation of their personal and professional lives.

Growth: At the foundational level, Growth aligns with the Root Chakra, grounding individuals like the roots of a tree. Just as a healthy root system ensures the stability of a tree, nurturing the Root Chakra becomes paramount for anchoring personal and professional development.

Guidance: Moving upward, Guidance resonates with the Sacral Chakra, the center of creativity and emotional balance. Like a mentor guiding a protégé, the Sacral Chakra channels the flow of guidance, encouraging individuals to tap into their creative energies and emotional intelligence for informed decision-making.

Grit: As we ascend, Grit finds resonance with the Solar Plexus Chakra, the seat of personal power. This chakra empowers individuals with the resilience to weather storms, much like a tree standing firm against adversities. Nurturing the Solar Plexus Chakra instills the determination needed to face professional challenges head-on.

Gallantry: The Heart Chakra, the center of compassion and ethical balance, embodies Gallantry in Premji's framework. Balancing ambition with compassion, the Heart Chakra guides individuals on a path of ethical conduct, fostering a harmonious and sustainable career journey.

Gratification: Moving higher, Gratification aligns with the Throat Chakra, the source of communication and expression. Just as a flower blooms, the Throat Chakra encourages individuals to express their achievements and joys, finding fulfillment not just in actions but in articulating the beauty of their journey.

Glow: The Third Eye Chakra, residing between the brows, resonates with Glow. This chakra symbolizes insight and intuition, fostering a positive mindset that illuminates the path ahead. Like the interconnectedness in nature, the Third Eye Chakra promotes collaboration, enabling individuals to shine collectively.

Greatness: At the pinnacle, Greatness corresponds to the Crown Chakra, the highest point of spiritual connection. This chakra transcends individual success, urging professionals to aspire for greatness that leaves a lasting legacy. Connecting with the Crown Chakra aligns individuals with a higher purpose, contributing to the collective 'greatness' of their professional realm.

In essence, Premji Boominathan's Transcendental Framework harmonizes with the 7 chakras, inviting individuals to embark on a transformative journey where personal and professional growth intertwines with the profound energies of the human body. The 7G Trail, guided by the wisdom of Growth, Guidance, Grit, Gallantry, Gratification, Glow, and Greatness, becomes a sacred odyssey, resonating with the symphony of chakras and the transcendence of one's holistic potential.

Reading this book is your first step of transformation towards your personal and professional success and fulfillment.

Introduction

"The Transcendental Professional" takes readers on a thrilling journey through the high-stakes world of gaming, innovation, and cultural transformation in India. At the heart of this narrative lies Cognos, a trailblazing gaming company on the verge of rewriting history with a groundbreaking algorithm. Their innovation promises to catapult India onto the global stage dominated by tech giants, yet internal strife threatens to derail their ambitions.

At the heart of Cognos' challenges lies a heated clash of egos and conflicting visions among department heads, evolving into a battleground that significantly shapes pivotal financial decisions. This internal discord hinders the transformative adaptation required in today's dynamic work environment, resulting in unmet expectations and hurdles in maintaining critical IT infrastructure. The tangible friction in decision-making casts a looming shadow over the company's foundational core. It is a high-stakes struggle for dominance and opposing ideas that urgently requires resolution to propel the organization forward in the ever-evolving landscape of the industry.

Enter Ramji, a visionary and transcendental professional renowned for his unconventional approach to leadership and problem-solving. With an unwavering commitment to change the trajectory of Cognos, Ramji undertakes the monumental task of bridging the chasm among stakeholders and guiding them toward a unified vision.

Ramji, through his unique 7G Transcendental Frameworke drawn from the natural laws of the forest and farm, principles steeped in wisdom and harmony with nature, guides the teams towards success. Through a series of transformative coaching sessions and strategic interventions, he challenges the entrenched beliefs and fosters a new ethos rooted in collaboration, innovation, and respect for individual perspectives.

As the narrative unfolds, readers witness the remarkable evolution of Cognos—from a company teetering on the brink of implosion to one poised for greatness. Ramji's mentorship not only revitalizes the company's culture but also instills a sense of purpose and unity among the team.

In the midst of the intense competition within the gaming landscape, Cognos embarked on a journey to unleash its collective potential, utilizing an innovative algorithm to secure a distinct competitive edge. Ramji's unconventional wisdom and teachings emerged as the guiding light, propelling Cognos toward unparalleled success.

"The Transcendental Professional" is a captivating tale of resilience, transformation, and the power of visionary leadership. It showcases the triumph of human spirit over adversity, illustrating how a harmonious blend of ancient wisdom and modern innovation can pave the way for a company—and a nation—to leave an indelible mark on the global stage.

Through the lens of Cognos' journey, this book serves as an inspiring testament to the possibilities that emerge when individuals embrace change, collaborate synergistically, and embrace a holistic approach to problem-solving—a lesson that extends far beyond the realms of gaming and into the fabric of societal progress.

After each episode, readers are invited to a reflective space, where the profound takeaways and attainments are laid bare. This postepisode revelation isn't just a summary—it's a key to unlocking a deeper understanding of the impact each twist and turn has on the characters and, by extension, the reader. Dive deep into the narrative, and you'll uncover the dynamic dance of the 7G Transcendental Framework, strategically applied by Ramji which directly or indirectly impacted the situation and the team in every episode.

"The Transcendental Professional" isn't merely a book; it's a transformative experience. Join us in this literary escapade, where fiction meets practicality, and every revelation is a stepping stone toward mastering the art of crisis management through the lens of Ramji's 7G Transcendental Framework. It's not just a story; it's an invitation to immerse yourself in a world of suspense, wisdom, and practical insights that will linger long after the final chapter.

Dynamic 7G Transcendental Framework

Growth (Spiral): Represents continuous development, expansion, and evolution, embodying perpetual progress and advancement.

Guidance (Compass Rose): Symbolizes direction, navigation, and the path to follow for wise counsel, offering clarity and purpose in decision-making.

Grit (Triangle): Signifies strength, resilience, and determination in the face of challenges, embodying unwavering perseverance and fortitude.

Gallantry (Pentagon): Represents courage, heroism, and noble behavior, exemplifying valor and integrity in all endeavors.

Gratification (Circles): Symbolizes fulfillment, satisfaction, and completeness, reflecting contentment and harmony in achievements and experiences.

Glow (Glowing circle): Radiates brightness, illumination, and brilliance, symbolizing inner light and external influence, inspiring others with its luminous presence.

Greatness (Hexagon): Signifies strength, unity, and the multifaceted nature of achieving greatness, embodying collective effort and exceptional achievement.

"Amidst the clamor of corporate challenges, in the very heart of confusion, anxiety, and worry, emerges a radiant beacon of hope—a transformative force that rises above the chaos, illuminating the path to unprecedented possibilities."

Episode #1:

Whispers of Change: The Arrival of the Enigmatic Pathfinder

In the dimly lit corner office of Cognos Solutions, Vishwa, the once-upbeat CEO, sat shrouded in an air of melancholy. His journey to this point had been an intense roller coaster of soaring triumphs and daunting trials, an odyssey that commenced with an audacious vision proposed by Aditi and brought to life by Vishwa. The vision is to craft a gaming algorithm so revolutionary, so awe-inspiring, that it would redefine the entire virtual gaming landscape.

With the fire of determination burning within, Aditi and Vishwa threw themselves into the development of this algorithm. Vishwa, having been a football player during his college days, was able to understand and build a strong case around Aditi's idea. They matured the concept into a vision, excluding Rohan from the brainstorming exercises as they believed it was still in the idea stage.

Little did they know that their decision to exclude Rohan, the Head of Technology, would later lead to a clash. The groundbreaking vision alone wasn't enough. The practicalities of bringing such a grand idea to fruition demanded resources – financial backing that could turn lines of code into a virtual masterpiece.

Undeterred, Vishwa stepped into the arena of potential investors, his confidence radiating like a beacon. With a passionate pitch and a compelling demonstration, he showcased the algorithm's transformative potential. And the investors were captivated – not just by the algorithm, but by Vishwa's unshakable conviction. Vishwa's momentous journey took a significant turn when his perfected gaming algorithm was ready to be unveiled to the world. His vision extended beyond just creating an innovative algorithm;

he aimed to reshape the entire virtual gaming landscape. With the financial backing secured from his investors, he was poised to take his brainchild to new heights.

In a surprising turn of events, Vishwa found himself at the crossroads of possibility. His investor, a silent ally in the background, unveiled a connection to the Virtual Gaming Federation, a powerhouse capable of turning his gaming vision into a tangible reality. Recognizing the potential embedded in Vishwa's algorithm, the investor saw an opportune moment to introduce it to the world.

This chance paved the way for Vishwa to stand before the prestigious Virtual Gaming Federation, an audience that could either make or break his groundbreaking gaming algorithm. As he prepared to present, the room pulsed with a collective sense of anticipation, transforming Vishwa from a mere CEO into a visionary on the brink of disrupting an entire industry.

A symphony of excitement and nerves played in his heart as Vishwa unfolded the meticulously crafted presentation. Each slide, each carefully chosen word, painted the evolutionary journey of his algorithm. It wasn't just a display of technical prowess; it was an immersion into a realm where gaming transcended boundaries.

Vishwa passionately conveyed that his creation wasn't limited to a specific game; it was a dynamic platform hosting a myriad of games, each promising an unprecedented level of engagement. With every demonstration, he wove a tapestry of a virtual gaming experience that went beyond borders, capturing the imagination of audiences globally.

The Virtual Gaming Federation's representatives sat captivated, drawn into the vision Vishwa was weaving. The potential of the algorithm resonated with their mission to push the limits of virtual gaming. As the presentation concluded, the room buzzed with excitement, discussions, and the promise of limitless possibilities.

The federation's representatives, visibly impressed and excited, voiced their unanimous approval. Vishwa stood at the epicenter of pride and disbelief. The federation's nod wasn't just a recognition of his algorithm's brilliance; it was an endorsement of his transformative vision. In that moment, he glimpsed a future where players worldwide would converge through virtual gaming, erasing geographical barriers in the name of digital camaraderie.

As the vibrant discussions unfolded, a thrilling strategy emerged, propelling the Virtual Gaming Platform into the spotlight with a spectacular launch, headlined by the exhilarating Virtual Football spectacle. Beyond the inaugural kickoff, the platform promised a personalized haven for players, complete with unique profiles, while coaches and managers could showcase their skills with dedicated profiles. Even clubs were invited to join the digital fray, laying the foundation for an epic league that would redefine virtual gaming.

The excitement escalated with the introduction of sponsorship registration options, adding an extra layer of anticipation to the grand launch was perfectly set for a groundbreaking revolution in the realm of virtual gaming.

"Imagine," Vishwa exclaimed, "a league that unites players, blurring the lines between casual and professional, in a virtual arena mirroring the thrill of real-world football tournaments."

According to the carefully crafted delivery road map and agreements in place, what had begun as a vision encoded in lines of software and fueled by unwavering determination had now transformed into something monumental. The Virtual Gaming Federation's approval stood as a testament to the potent combination of innovation and collaboration. Vishwa's algorithm was poised to command the global stage in a gaming revolution, and as he absorbed the magnitude of the moment, he couldn't help but marvel at the extraordinary journey that had led him to this pivotal point.

The Press release the following week released by Cognos and Virtual Gaming Federation captured the stakes:

"Two industry leaders, Cognos and the Virtual Gaming Federation (VGF), are thrilled to announce a strategic collaboration that promises to make waves in the world of Virtual gaming. This partnership brings together the technical expertise of Cognos and the gaming prowess of VGF to deliver an unparalleled gaming experience.

Cognos, a renowned technology partner, will play a pivotal role in this venture. Their cutting-edge solutions and technical acumen will provide a solid foundation for the gaming experiences to come, while the Virtual Gaming Federation will leverage its extensive knowledge in competitive gaming events and community engagement.

"We're excited to embark on this journey with the Virtual Gaming Federation. Cognos, as the technology partner, will provide the innovative solutions needed to create a gaming environment that sets new industry standards," said Vishwa, CEO at Cognos. He continued, "Together with VGF, we aim to offer gamers a platform where they can not only compete but also connect, excel, and enjoy a unique gaming world."

The Federation's audacious vision had set the stage for an exhilarating journey, but it came with a tight timeline – just 12 months to bring the virtual football league to life. Vishwa understood that the clock was ticking, and the pressure to deliver was immense.

As investors, they would undoubtedly exert pressure to release early and deliver iteratively. With that in mind, Vishwa decided to revise the project timeline.

The MVP [Minimum Viable Product] would be brought forward to 90 days from the project's inception, aligning with the investors' expectations as the investors suggested that they need an MVP before the funds can be released based on the delivery. By making these adjustments, Vishwa hoped to strike a balance between meeting investor expectations and maintaining the quality and functionality of the virtual football league.

The potential billion-dollar revenue stream awaiting Cognos Solutions marked a monumental opportunity to redefine the gaming industry. This pursuit wasn't a gamble but a meticulously calculated journey toward success, where every digit held the promise of transforming the landscape.

The team raced against time, each passing hour a relentless reminder of the narrow margin for error. These hours weren't mere ticks of the clock; they were a countdown echoing through the corridors, urging precision and unwavering punctuality.

Within this numerical realm, financial boundaries constrained the visionary dreams, tethered by a $50 million budget that demanded exacting allocation. Every digit in this financial equation represented an opportunity, a balancing act between innovation and fiscal prudence.

Yet, these numbers weren't just indicators of potential revenue; they embodied risks and challenges inherent in this ambitious venture.

In the intricate web of development, the proposed 100+ features weren't mere additions; they embodied the potential to redefine the gaming experience. Each digit in this count symbolized rigorous scrutiny for their impact on system stability and the ultimate user experience.

The press encapsulated the situation in their headlines:

"Unraveling the High-Stakes Numbers: *Pioneering the Future of Virtual Gaming"*

"10 Million Gamers: *The Billion-Dollar Wager on Cognos Solutions' Launch"*

In the pulsating realm of the gaming industry, Cognos Solutions emerged as a dynamic player ready to make waves. With a staggering 3 billion gamers scattered across the globe, the competitive battleground, while currently dominated by the United States and China, awaited a global uprising. The allure of exhilarating virtual experiences was set to transcend borders, promising a seismic shift in the gaming landscape.

In this exhilarating arena, where the boundary between virtual and real dissolves, Cognos Solutions positioned itself for an unprecedented impact. Projections painted a vivid picture of the eSports industry's trajectory, forecasting a surge to $2 billion by 2024. However, the excitement didn't stop there; the stakes were bound to catapult to an astronomical $6 to $12 billion by the illustrious horizon of 2030. The narrative unfolded as a testament to the escalating intensity in a domain where organized gaming was crafting the blueprint for the future—a future brimming with boundless possibilities and infinite digital adventures.

However, the narrative extended beyond mere technicalities. It cantered on capturing the imagination of gamers and investors, instilling confidence that beckoned support from the burgeoning Virtual Gaming Foundation and other key investors.

Eager to rise to the challenge, Vishwa embarked on a hiring spree. Cognos Solutions transitioned from a small, tightly-knit group of dedicated geeks into a sprawling organization with hundreds of employees. Engineers, designers, content creators, and administrators were all brought on board to contribute their skills and expertise to the monumental task at hand.

However, as the organization expanded, so did the complexities. What started as small disagreements between Heads of Departments gradually evolved into something far more complex – a clash of egos and a battle for dominance among various departments. Among the key players in this unfolding drama were Aditi Sharma, the passionate and ambitious Product Head; Rohan Kapoor, the analytical and perfectionist Technical Head; Aakash Gupta, the calm and diplomatic Accounts Head; and Maya Patel, the empathetic and strategic HR Head.

Aditi was a force of nature, known for her relentless determination and unwavering belief in enhancing user experiences. She had an innate ability to envision features that would captivate players and revolutionize the gaming landscape. Her fiery enthusiasm was fueled by her history of overcoming obstacles, and she saw the virtual football league as an opportunity to redefine how people experienced gaming. Aditi was a dreamer, always pushing the boundaries of what was possible.

Rohan, on the other hand, possessed an analytical mind that could decipher complex codes as effortlessly as others read a book. His commitment to stability, reliability, scalability, availability and security stemmed from his deep-rooted perfectionism.

He approached challenges with caution, fearing failure and obsessing over precision. For him, the technical feasibility of implementing Aditi's innovative ideas was a serious concern. He couldn't afford to compromise the company's reputation by rushing something that might lead to technical glitches.

Amidst the clash of ideas between Aditi and Rohan, Aakash Gupta, the Accounts Head, found himself caught in the crossfire. Aakash had a reputation for his knack with numbers and his ability to navigate tricky financial situations with grace. However, the clash of egos between the product and technical departments had direct implications on resource allocation and budgeting. He was tasked with finding the delicate balance between funding Aditi's innovative features and Rohan's need for technical stability.

Maya Patel, the HR Head, was rooted in the conventional methods of HR management, which, didn't emphasize transformation or change.

Sourav, the IT Infrastructure Head, was a character who consistently approached his role with skepticism when it came to IT resource allocation. His primary focus always seemed to be on cost savings rather than optimizing the resource requirements based on the technical team's input.

Sourav had a tendency to dismiss the technical team's recommendations, preferring to rely on his own understanding and decisions. He rarely engaged in discussions about the technical architecture or requirements with the rest of the team.

This created significant conflicts within the IT department, as the team's expectations and needs were often left unfulfilled.

Sourav's approach to resource allocation and cost savings clashed with the technical team's desire for a more collaborative and technically sound approach.

This ongoing conflict was a source of tension and frustration within the department, as it hindered their ability to effectively implement and maintain IT infrastructure that met the organization's needs and industry standards.

Aditi's relentless drive to introduce cutting-edge features collided with Rohan's technical apprehensions, setting off shock waves throughout the company. What were once occasional disagreements in meetings now unfolded as fierce battlegrounds of contrasting opinions and escalating tensions. The clash between the product and technical departments resonated through the corridors, unsettling the very foundation of the company.

As the buzz around the proposal for the virtual football league intensified, the ambitions of each department soared, fueling a palpable sense of rivalry. Amidst this escalating excitement, Aakash grappled with the complex challenge of allocating resources effectively.

Meanwhile, the struggle between data security and user convenience escalated, highlighting the delicate balance that Cognos was striving to achieve. Rohan's insistence on strict security measures was a reaction of his deep concern for safeguarding user data. He knew that a single breach could have far-reaching consequences.

Aditi, driven by her commitment to seamless user experiences, worried about complicating the process for users. She saw the potential risk of alienating users with a cumbersome process and believed in striking the right balance between security and ease.

As the pressure mounted, Maya found herself navigating the increasingly tense relationships among the departments. She recognized the importance of maintaining a united front and addressing conflicts before they escalated. She initiated team-building workshops, one-on-one sessions, and open forums for communication, all in an effort to bridge the widening gaps and restore the collaborative spirit that had once defined Cognos Solutions.

In the midst of intensifying clashes and rising tension, a new figure emerged in the story – the Chief Financial Officer, Rajesh Malhotra. With a sharp mind for numbers and an uncanny ability to cut costs, Rajesh had joined Cognos Solutions just months before the countdown to the virtual football league launch began. He was known for his meticulous attention to financial details, but his tunnel vision for cost-cutting sometimes led him to lose sight of the bigger picture.

Rajesh, hailing from a traditional industry background, was a self-proclaimed master of spreadsheets and budget analysis. He had a reputation for approaching every decision with a laser focus on the bottom line, a trait deeply ingrained in his traditional industry experience.

Rajesh's introduction to the organization sent ripples through the workforce. Employees soon realized that every financial aspect would be subjected to his meticulous scrutiny. His traditional industry background influenced his financial approach, and he was often seen as the embodiment of stringent financial control and efficiency.

With a good financial domain background, Rajesh brought a unique perspective to the table. He was notorious for scrutinizing even the smallest expenses and was known to engage in lengthy debates over the necessity of seemingly trivial purchases. While his approach undoubtedly saved the company money, it also raised eyebrows and occasionally generated frustration among his colleagues.

However, his relentless pursuit of financial efficiency sometimes caused him to overlook the broader context. Vishwa, the CEO, often found himself in heated discussions with Rajesh about the necessity of investing in innovative ideas that could propel the company's growth. Rajesh's obsession with cost- cutting sometimes clouded his ability to see the potential returns that could arise from strategic investments.

As the clashes between departments escalated, Rajesh's financial arguments often clashed head-on with Aditi's and Rohan's visionary perspectives. His skepticism about spending on creative initiatives frequently put him at odds with Aditi's passion for innovation and Rohan's technical aspirations. The clash between Rajesh's numbers-driven approach and the creative minds' ambitions was a recurring theme in the company's decision-making process.

Vishwa recognized the value of Rajesh's financial acumen, especially in an environment where resources were being stretched thin. However, he also grappled with the challenge of striking a balance between fiscal responsibility and the need to pursue bold, game-changing projects.

With less than 12 Months left until the virtual football league's launch, the Cognos Solutions office became a battleground of opinions and tensions. The clash between Aditi's passion and Rohan's caution reverberated through the corridors, threatening to tear the company apart. The push for innovation clashed with concerns of technical readiness. The need for security clashed with the desire for user convenience.

During this turmoil, Vishwa's own anxiety intensified. He watched as the company he had nurtured with so much care began to unravel under the weight of internal conflicts.

The workplace culture was eroding, and he saw the hollowing effects it was having on the company's collective spirit. He knew that something had to change – something unconventional that could mend the fractures and realign the company's focus on the shared goal of success.

Amid the swirling challenges that surrounded Cognos Solutions, Vishwa found himself seeking solace in the company of a trusted friend and fellow entrepreneur, Rajat.

Rajat was not only the owner of a successful IT company but also someone Vishwa had known for years. Their friendship had weathered the storms of entrepreneurship, and now, as Vishwa grappled with the turmoil at Cognos, he turned to Rajat for guidance.

One evening, as they sat across from each other at a cozy cafe, the conversation naturally veered toward the struggles Vishwa was facing. The weight of responsibility hung heavily on his shoulders, and he candidly shared the internal conflicts, the escalating tensions, and the impending launch of the virtual football league – a launch that seemed to grow more uncertain with each passing day.

Rajat listened intently, his empathetic gaze never leaving Vishwa's eyes. He understood the immense pressure that came with running a company, the sleepless nights, and the relentless pursuit of success. As Vishwa poured his heart out, Rajat's face suddenly lit up with a knowing smile, as if a solution had just presented itself.

"You know, Vishwa," Rajat began, his voice carrying a sense of excitement, "I've been through my fair share of challenges in the business world. And I've seen companies struggling with execution, much like what you're describing with Cognos. But let me tell you about someone who has the power to transform even the direst situations. Rajat leaned forward, his voice lowered as if sharing a well-kept secret. "His name is Ramji," he revealed, his words carrying an air of reverence. "Ramji is not your ordinary coach or consultant. He's an enigma, someone who has developed a powerful framework called "The 7G Transcendental Framework" that has breathed new life into struggling companies."

Transcendental professionals, known for their exceptional expertise and wisdom, offer valuable support in various ways. They serve as mentors, sharing insights on career development and decision-making, provide knowledge transfer through workshops, assist in problem-solving, offer networking opportunities, and provide emotional support. They inspire and motivate others, contribute to thought leadership, aid in strategic planning, facilitate conflict resolution, and leave a legacy by mentoring and passing on their wisdom to future generations.

Intrigued, Vishwa leaned in closer, his focus solely on Rajat's words. "Tell me more about Ramji and his framework" he urged.

Rajat's eyes sparkled as he began recounting stories of companies that were struggling on the brink of collapse, much like Cognos Solutions.

He recalled that one notable success story that exemplifies the effectiveness of Ramji's 'Transcendental Framework: Advancing along the 7G Trail - Growth, Guidance, Grit, Gallantry, Gratification, Glow, and Greatness' involves a company in the financial services sector, "Infinite Financial Solutions." At the time Ramji was brought in, the company was facing significant challenges. It suffered from a silo-ed organizational structure, communication breakdowns, and a lack of alignment among teams and departments. The company was on the verge of losing valuable clients and had a declining reputation in the market.

Ramji, with his unique approach, started by conducting in-depth assessments and interviews across all levels of the organization. He emphasized the importance of open and honest communication, encouraging employees to voice their concerns, ideas, and aspirations. Through this process, he identified underlying cultural issues and recognized the potential for transformation.

Ramji introduced a series of interventions aimed at reshaping the company's culture and processes. He implemented engaging workshops where managers were guided to adopt a more inclusive and empathetic approach. Additionally, he introduced cross-functional teamwork, breaking down departmental silos and fostering collaboration.

Over time, the effects of Ramji's framework became evident. Infinite Financial Solutions witnessed a remarkable turnaround. The company's employees became more engaged, working cohesively toward a common purpose. Communication barriers dissolved, and a culture of transparency and innovation emerged. As a result, the company's client satisfaction rates improved, and they began to secure new business opportunities.

In just a couple of years, Infinite Financial Solutions not only regained its market standing but also emerged as a model of organizational transformation in the financial services sector. This success story illustrates how Ramji's unique blend of psychology, leadership principles, and unorthodox strategies can bring about profound and positive changes in even the most challenging business environments. Rajath described how Ramji had an uncanny ability to diagnose the root causes of problems, unraveling complex organizational knots that others deemed unsolvable.

"But what truly sets Ramji apart is his transformational framework," Rajat continued. "He doesn't just address surface-level issues; he delves deep into the core of a company's culture, values, and processes. And through a series of carefully curated interventions, he empowers teams to break down silos, align their goals, and work towards a common purpose."

Vishwa's gaze remained fixed on Rajat, absorbing every detail. "How does he do it?" he asked, his curiosity now fully ignited.

Rajat animatedly described Ramji's framework as a captivating fusion of psychology, leadership principles inspired by nature, and a repertoire of unorthodox strategies. "Ramji's philosophy is rooted in the belief that genuine transformation commences with a shift in mindset. He thrives on challenging conventional thinking, disrupting established hierarchies, and fostering a culture of open communication. While his methods might seem unconventional, the results they yield are nothing short of extraordinary."

As Rajat shared more stories of companies that had undergone remarkable turnarounds under Ramji's guidance, Vishwa felt a glimmer of hope ignite within him. The challenges at Cognos seemed insurmountable, but the idea of a transformative force like Ramji was a beacon of possibility.

"Rajat," Vishwa exclaimed, his voice echoing with a blend of hope and determination, "can you imagine the impact Ramji could make for us at Cognos?"

Rajat nodded, a knowing smile on his lips. "Absolutely, Vishwa. It won't be an easy journey as he charges a premium for his assignments, but if anyone can guide Cognos through this, it's Ramji."

As the evening sun set and the cafe's lights cast a warm glow around them, Vishwa's mind was abuzz with thoughts of Ramji and the possibility of transformation. The stories he had heard painted a vivid picture of a path forward – a path that promised unity, collaboration, and success. With renewed determination, Vishwa thanked Rajat for his invaluable insights, knowing that he was now armed with a potential solution to the challenges that had seemed insurmountable.

With Rajat's words about Ramji echoing in his mind, Vishwa returned to Cognos Solutions with a newfound determination. He had a proposal that could potentially reshape the fate of the company, but he knew that presenting it to his team and the board wouldn't be easy.

Gathering his team in a conference room, Vishwa took a deep breath and began to share the story of Ramji – the enigmatic coach who had transformed struggling companies into success stories. As he spoke about Ramji's unique framework and the remarkable turnarounds he had facilitated, he could sense the skepticism in the room.

Aditi, the passionate Product Head, was the first to voice her doubts. "Vishwa, it sounds too good to be true," she said with a furrowed brow. "How can someone come in and change the course of our company in just a few months? Our challenges run deep, and our internal conflicts are complex."

Rohan, the analytical Technical Head, chimed in. "And what about the technical feasibility? We can't afford disruptions in the current setup. We can't just overhaul our processes without careful consideration."

The pragmatic Accounts Head, raised his concerns again about the financial aspect. "Vishwa, you know we're already stretched in terms of budget. Bringing in this Ramji – what's his cost? You mentioned he commands a premium in the market? Can we really justify the expense, especially if there's no guarantee of success?"

Maya, the HR Head, added, "And what about the team dynamics? Introducing an outsider could exacerbate tensions even further. We're already dealing with clashes between departments. Will Ramji's presence add fuel to the fire?"

Vishwa listened to their concerns, his heart heavy with the weight of their doubts. He understood their reservations – after all, the idea of a transformative change within a short time seemed like a lofty goal. But he also believed that Cognos Solutions had reached a critical juncture, where unconventional measures were necessary.

"I hear your concerns," Vishwa finally said, his voice steady. "I understand that this is a bold step, and it's not without risks. But consider this: we're on the brink of a major launch – The Virtual Gaming Platform that could redefine our company. We can't afford to stumble due to internal conflicts.

He looked around the room, meeting the eyes of each team member. "Ramji's track record speaks for itself. He's not just an ordinary consultant. He has transformed companies facing even worse challenges than ours. Yes, there's a cost involved, but think about the potential return on investment. If Ramji can guide us to a successful launch, the benefits could be immeasurable."

The room crackled with the energy of a passionate debate, voices clashing and rebounding off the walls. In the midst of the fervor, Vishwa's attentive ears absorbed every argument, his mind sprinting through the maze of pros and cons. As the echoes of debate settled, the weight of the decision descended squarely onto his shoulders, a realization that hung in the air.

Taking a deep breath, he looked at his team with a determined expression. "I've made up my mind," he announced. "I believe in the potential of Ramji's framework. Yes, there are risks, but the potential rewards are too great to ignore. We're bringing him in. We're giving ourselves a chance to not only succeed with The Virtual Gaming Platform but also to transform our company's culture."

The room fell silent, the weight of Vishwa's decision sinking in. Despite the doubts and uncertainties, there was a sense of anticipation in the air – the anticipation of change, of possibility, of a new path forward.

As Vishwa exited the conference room, he felt the thrill of the upcoming journey coursing through his veins. Introducing Ramji promised to be an exhilarating challenge, and steering through the intricate dynamics between the team and the enigmatic coach demanded a finesse that Vishwa was eager to master. Fueled by stories of profound transformations, captivated by the potential of a fresh perspective, and animated by the vision of a radiant future for Cognos Solutions, Vishwa was ready to embark on an adventure of change and renewal.

The corridors buzzed with hushed conversations, speculations swirling like a storm of curiosity. As Ramji's impending arrival drew nearer, debates ignited, and opinions clashed. Some were excited by the prospect of change, while others held onto skepticism, unsure of how an outsider could transform their deeply rooted dynamics.

The much-anticipated moment dawned, and the boardroom hummed with eager excitement. Every gaze was riveted, hearts beating in anticipation, as the door dramatically swung open.

And there he was – a captivating embodiment of mystery and authority. A hush enveloped the room, signaling the beginning of a mesmerizing new chapter for Cognos.

"As we stand at the precipice of uncertainty, skepticism lingers in the air. Yet, within the heart of adversity, there sparks the ember of potential—a hopeful journey waiting to unfold. The journey begins, and it is one of unwavering hope, resolute determination, and the audacity to redefine what success truly means."

Episode #2:

Harmony at Dawn: The Symphony of Transformation Begins

Ramji entered the boardroom with a calm and composed demeanor, his presence commanding attention and respect. Vishwa introduced him to the team, his voice laced with a mixture of hope and excitement. As Ramji began to speak, his words carried an air of wisdom and authority.

"Thank you all for having me here," Ramji began, his gaze sweeping across the room.

"I acknowledge the complexity and depth of the challenges you're navigating, and my approach is one of understanding rather than judgment. I'm committed to conducting a comprehensive review with all teams to gain insights into the current situation and establish a baseline. I firmly believe that genuine transformation occurs when we courageously venture beyond our comfort zones, welcoming fresh perspectives into our collective journey."

His words hung in the air, a pregnant pause that seemed to echo through the room. Aditi, Rohan, Aakash, and Maya exchanged glances, each processing Ramji's presence in their own way.

Ramji continued, "I've been privileged to work with companies that are facing challenging environments, just like Cognos is now. And I've seen firsthand the power of collaboration, empathy, and a shared sense of purpose in turning things around."

He walked to the whiteboard and began sketching a diagram that illustrated the interconnectedness of the company's departments. "Imagine this as our company's ecosystem," he explained. "Every department plays a crucial role, and when these departments are in harmony, the entire system flourishes."

Aditi leaned forward, her curiosity evident. "But our departments have been at each other, and that's causing discord," she interjected.

Ramji nodded, acknowledging her concern. "That's true, Aditi. And that's where my framework comes in. It's not just about addressing the surface-level conflicts; it's about uncovering the underlying beliefs, values, and dynamics that fuel these conflicts."

As Ramji spoke, a new understanding seemed to dawn on the faces of the team members. He went on to describe his approach – a series of workshops, dialogues, and exercises designed to break down silos, encourage open communication, and foster a culture of collaboration. Rohan's analytical mind was still skeptical. "How do we ensure that this doesn't disrupt our ongoing projects?" he asked.

Ramji smiled. "I understand your concern, Rohan. The workshops and interventions will be carefully curated to minimize disruptions. In fact, my goal is to enhance the efficiency of your processes by aligning them with the company's shared vision."

Aakash chimed in, his diplomatic nature evident. "And what about the financial aspect? We're already working with a tight budget."

Ramji's gaze shifted to Aakash. "I appreciate your concern, Aakash. My approach is not about extravagant spending. It's about channeling resources towards initiatives that drive growth and innovation. The return on investment often outweighs the initial costs."

Ramji's demeanor shifted into a contemplative mode. "A pivotal element in our journey revolves around forging a secure haven where everyone can freely voice their opinions, be truly listened to, and acknowledge the unique strengths each department brings to the table."

Vishwa watched as Ramji's words resonated with his team. There was a shift in the atmosphere of the room – a sense of possibility, a glimmer of hope. "We're not looking for a quick fix," Ramji emphasized. "This journey will require dedication, patience, and a willingness to embrace change. But I firmly believe that when a company aligns its values, its processes, and its people, it can overcome even the most daunting challenges.

"Do any of you play a musical instrument?"

A sense of bewilderment washed over the team members as they looked around, unsure of how this question was relevant to their current predicament. Nonetheless, a few hesitant hands tentatively rose.

Ramji's smile widened. "Perfect," he exclaimed. "But before we dive into our musical adventure, let me assure you that there is a deeper meaning to this exercise. Curiosity mingled with skepticism as the team members contemplated Ramji's words. The atmosphere in the room remained uncertain, the weight of their challenges still pressing upon them.

"Now, let us embark on a musical journey," Ramji declared, his eyes gleaming with excitement. "But first, let's find our orchestrator " and he looked at Vishwa.

Vishwa's eyes widened as Ramji's words hung in the air. He hadn't anticipated this turn of events. The role of an orchestrator intrigued him, and he could feel a sense of anticipation building in the room. With a nod, he stepped forward, embracing the challenge that lay ahead.

"Vishwa, I want you to stand in the centre of the room," Ramji instructed, his voice gentle yet commanding. Vishwa complied, positioning himself amidst the expectant faces of his team members.

"Team," Ramji addressed the group with a vibrant energy. Placing a speaker on the table, he orchestrated the excitement by dividing the team into 5 groups. With a touch of musical flair, he declared, "Listen closely to the unique melody of each instrument. Choose one for your group. Let's kick off with the Piano," and played its enchanting tune. As he assigned each group their musical companion – the Violin, the Drums, the Trumpet, and the Harp – anticipation filled the room. Bursting with enthusiasm, he inquired, "How do these instruments sound individually?" The resounding response echoed, "Sounded good!"

Ramji declared, "Vishwa here is our orchestrator, responsible for bringing all these instruments together in harmony. Now all close your eyes"

"Consider yourselves as musical experts, each wielding a distinct instrument of leadership. In this symphony of success, the key is harmonizing your instruments, synchronizing the rhythm and melody. It's not about one instrument taking the spotlight; it's about crafting a harmonious and unified masterpiece together."

With his eyes closed, Vishwa could feel the weight of Ramji's words sinking in. The metaphor resonated deeply with the challenges they were facing – the clash of egos, the dominance battles, and the need for collaboration.

Ramji played a mesmerizing symphony, seamlessly blending all the allocated instruments. "Now, envision each of you playing your designated instrument," Ramji encouraged. "Feel the reverberations, the enchanting melodies, and the harmonious fusion. Listen keenly to your instrument and those of your fellow musicians, adapt to the evolving rhythms, and discover your unique place in this beautiful composition."

As Ramji's voice trailed off, Vishwa's senses heightened. He could hear the blend of diverse instruments coming together in a harmonious arrangement.

Slowly, he began to hear the soft rustling of movement as his team members, eyes still closed, started to mimic the act of playing their instruments.

The room was enveloped in a serene stillness, broken only by the sounds of the symphony. As the moments passed, the played music grew more cohesive, as if the team members were tuning into a rhythm that bound them together.

Ramji skillfully elevated the symphony's volume, infusing it with heightened intensity. Then, as if prompted by an unspoken signal, he shared his wisdom, "Keep tuning in to the instruments surrounding you. Allow the melodies to entwine, and let the sweet harmony emerge from the unity of your collective efforts.

As Ramji spoke, the melody crescendo-ed in Vishwa's thoughts. The room pulsed with energy, a collective dedication resonating to craft something extraordinary out of the harmonious blend of sounds.

As the music grew louder, Vishwa felt a profound connection with his team. The barriers that had divided them seemed to dissolve, replaced by a sense of camaraderie and shared purpose. The symphony was no longer just a metaphor - it had become a manifestation of their potential to work together in harmony.

Ramji allowed the music to gently fade into the background, and with a serene smile, he guided, "As you open your eyes, let's gracefully return to the beauty of the present moment."

As the team members slowly opened their eyes, the room was filled with a sense of wonder and unity. Vishwa looked around, and he could see it in their faces - a realization that they were all part of a larger whole, that their individual strengths could combine to create something extraordinary.

As the exercise concludes, Ramji debriefs the team, "It sounded good when each instrument was played separately. But, then played as a composition, it was mind-blowing. And that, my friends, connects to the point." The boardroom, once a space for business discussions, had transformed into a symphony theater, resonating with the live performance of their collaborative efforts.

Ramji smiled, his gaze moving from one team member to another. "You see," he said softly, "just like in a symphony, each instrument has its unique voice, and when they come together, they create magic. In our journey ahead, we are those instruments, and together, we have the power to create something truly remarkable."

The room was filled with a renewed sense of purpose, the doubts and uncertainties of moments ago replaced by a newfound hope.

Vishwa felt a surge of gratitude for Rajat's introduction to Ramji, for the spark of possibility that had been ignited.

Ramji's gaze swept across the room, his eyes meeting the curious and expectant looks of the team members. The air was charged with a mixture of skepticism and intrigue, a palpable energy that hung in anticipation of his next words.

"In the upcoming days," Ramji declared, his voice unwavering and filled with confidence, "we're diving into a series of workshops that defy the ordinary. These sessions aren't here to disrupt your workflow but to elevate it to new heights."

His words sparked a blend of raised eyebrows and exchanged glances among the team. The notion of workshops contributing to their work rather than disrupting it was a novel and intriguing concept, leaving the team uncertain yet curious about Ramji's assertion.

Ramji continued, his expression unwavering. "You see, these workshops are not meant to be detached from your daily responsibilities. Instead, they will be intricately woven into the fabric of your projects, your collaborations, and your goals. They will serve as catalysts for change, sparking new ideas, fostering collaboration, and facilitating the alignment of our efforts."

He paused for a moment, allowing his words to sink in before he elaborated further. "Each workshop will be designed to address specific challenges, to uncover underlying dynamics, and to provide practical tools that you can immediately apply to your work. It's not about theoretical concepts that remain in isolation – it's about actionable insights that will propel us forward."

Vishwa watched as the team members exchanged glances once again, this time with a sense of intrigue mingled with a growing willingness to embrace the unknown. The promise of workshops that would enhance their work rather than disrupt it seemed to be striking a chord.

Ramji's eyes locked onto Aditi, who had been among the most vocal skeptics earlier. Aditi," he said, his tone gentle yet resolute, "consider if one of our shared objectives is to enhance user experience. Imagine if we could channel your passion for elevating user experiences into our ongoing projects, using the insights from these workshops to further enhance the engagement and immersion of our players. Envision how the technical solutions Rohan envisions could be even more seamlessly integrated, thanks to the collaborative environment these workshops will foster."

Aditi's expression softened, a glimmer of possibility entering her eyes. The notion of her ideas finding a practical outlet within the company's projects seemed like a dream she hadn't dared to hope for.

Rohan, too, seemed to be considering the implications of Ramji's words. "Rohan," Ramji addressed him, "think of how the technical feasibility you value so much can be enriched by a holistic understanding of the entire process. These workshops will provide us with a platform to address concerns and streamline processes, ensuring that technical stability and innovation coexist."

Rohan's analytical mind seemed to be processing this new perspective, the boundaries between innovation and stability beginning to blur.

"Aakash," Ramji turned to the Finance Head, "imagine how these workshops can offer insights into efficient resource allocation, optimizing our budget to support both innovation and stability. The financial aspect need not be a barrier; it can be a facilitator of growth."

Aakash nodded thoughtfully, the potential alignment of financial strategy with the company's broader goals resonating with his practical sensibilities.

Ramji's gaze swept across the room once more, his presence commanding attention and respect. "Team, The first workshop starts at 6 am in the conference room tomorrow and you will be ready for work by 9:30 am before the start of your work day with the key insights…

The prospect of early morning workshops, however, raised a few eyebrows and shocked a few who work late in the night. The idea of starting the day well before the usual work hours wasn't something that everyone was willing to embrace.

Ramji's expression remained unwavering as he addressed the unspoken concerns. "I understand that early mornings might not be everyone's preference," he continued, "but let me assure you, this is worth it. Early mornings provide the clarity and stillness that can set the tone for a productive day. The world is quieter, distractions are minimized, and your mind is more receptive to insights that might elude you during the busier hours."

Vishwa watched as Ramji's words seemed to be weaving a tapestry of possibilities, connecting each team member's strengths with the promise of the upcoming workshops. The once-skeptical atmosphere was now evolving into a sense of curiosity and anticipation.

Vishwa could see the team members processing Ramji's words, their skepticism giving way to a growing curiosity. The promise of a new perspective, of insights that could potentially transform their approach to work, seemed to be kindling a spark within them.

"Moreover," Ramji added with a warm smile, "by starting our workshops early, we're sending a collective message to ourselves – that we're committed to embracing change, to pushing our boundaries, and to embarking on this journey together. The dedication you show to these early morning sessions will set the rhythm for our symphony of change."

As Ramji's words settled, Vishwa could sense a shift in the room's atmosphere. The initial reluctance was beginning to yield to a sense of purpose, a recognition that these early morning workshops might just be the catalyst they needed to harmonize their efforts and bring about the transformation they sought.

The next morning dawned with an air of anticipation, and as the team members gathered outside the conference room, a sense of curiosity buzzed in the air. Little did they know that what awaited them inside would be a sight that left them utterly amazed and intrigued, setting the stage for a chapter of transformation unlike any they had experienced before. Some were still rubbing the sleep from their eyes, holding their cups of coffee like a lifeline. Others arrived with the energy of a morning workout, ready to tackle whatever lay ahead. As the doors swung open and they entered the room, their tiredness and morning routines were quickly forgotten, replaced by a scene that defied their expectations.

Takeaways

- **Embrace of New Perspectives:** *Belief that true transformation requires stepping outside comfort zones and embracing new perspectives.*

- **Power of Collaboration and Empathy:** *Transformative power of collaboration, empathy, and shared purpose in turning around challenging environments.*

- **Systemic Approach to Company Ecosystems:** *Systemic view of the company's departments, emphasizing their interconnectedness and the need for harmony.*

- **Addressing Underlying Dynamics:** *Importance of addressing underlying beliefs, values, and dynamics that fuel conflicts, not just surface-level issues.*

- **Efficiency Enhancement through Alignment:** *Goal to enhance efficiency by aligning processes with the company's shared vision.*

- **Financial Resource Channeling:** *Addressing concerns about the budget by focusing on channeling resources toward initiatives that drive growth and innovation.*

- **Building a Secure Haven for Communication:** *Creating a secure environment for open communication, where everyone's opinions are valued.*

- **Metaphorical Learning through Music:** *Utilizing a metaphorical approach using a musical symphony to convey the importance of harmonizing diverse strengths.*

Attainments

- **Transformation of Atmosphere:** *Transforming the boardroom atmosphere from skepticism and uncertainty to one filled with possibility, hope, and renewed purpose.*

- **Formation of a Unified Team:** *Successfully bringing the team together through the musical exercise, breaking down barriers, and fostering a sense of camaraderie.*

- **Introduction of Workshop Concept:** *Introducing a novel concept of workshops intricately woven into daily responsibilities to spark new ideas, foster collaboration, and align efforts.*

- **Alignment of Workshops with Projects:** *Aligning workshops with ongoing projects, promising practical tools to address challenges and uncover underlying dynamics.*

- **Changing Perspectives of Team Members:** *Successfully shifting the perspectives of skeptical team members, making them more open to the idea of workshops enhancing their work.*

Applying the Dynamic 7G Transcendental Framework

Growth:

Learning Orientation: *Encouraging a learning orientation by introducing new perspectives and transformative approaches.*

Organizational Growth: *Aiming at enhancing the company's growth through collaborative efforts and alignment with shared visions.*

Guidance:

Systemic Guidance: *Providing guidance on systemic issues within the company, addressing underlying dynamics and conflicts.*

Practical Guidance: *Offering practical guidance on conducting workshops seamlessly integrated into daily responsibilities.*

Grit:

Overcoming Challenges: *Acknowledging and addressing concerns raised by team members, demonstrating grit in overcoming skepticism and resistance.*

Commitment to Early Morning Workshops: *Encouraging a commitment to early morning workshops as a symbol of dedication and perseverance.*

Gallantry:

Bold Approach to Transformation: *Demonstrating gallantry by introducing bold and transformative approaches, such as using a musical metaphor for team building.*

Gratitude:

Acknowledgment of Concerns: *Showing gratitude by acknowledging financial concerns and assuring the team of a focused and beneficial resource allocation.*

Appreciation for Team's Dedication: *Expressing gratitude for the team's dedication to early morning sessions, highlighting its significance in the journey of change.*

Glow:

Creation of Positive Atmosphere: *Creating a positive atmosphere in the boardroom, replacing doubts with hope and skepticism with curiosity.*

Elevating Team's Energy: *Elevating the team's energy through the musical exercise, infusing a sense of wonder and unity.*

Greatness:

Transformational Leadership: *Embodying greatness through transformational leadership, inspiring the team to envision and strive for something truly remarkable.*

Setting the Stage for Extraordinary Transformation: *Setting the stage for greatness by introducing workshops that promise to be catalysts for change and transformation.*

"In the grand tapestry of success, strength thrives in interdependence. As transcendental professionals, embracing the undeniable truth of our intricate connections propels us forward. A legacy of collective growth unfolds, transcending the boundaries of singular achievement. Bound by ties unspoken, a symphony arises—echoing strength, efficiency, and swift ascension."

Episode #3:

Ramji's Transformative Symphony: A Profound Crescendo into Professional Excellence

The conference room was bathed in the soft morning light as Ramji stood at the front of the room, the embodiment of calm and purpose, poised to guide them through a profound exploration.

With a sense of purpose, Ramji initiated the conversation by visiting Stephen Covey's principle: *"You have to be independent before you can become interdependent."*

"This mantra had become a lodestar, guiding their exploration of collaboration's depth. The room buzzed with curiosity as Ramji delved into the intricate nuances of their childhood years."

"Think back to when we were children," he began. "We were vulnerable and dependent on our caregivers for everything – from our basic needs to emotional support. As we grew, there was a burning desire to shed our dependence and become 'big kids.' Independence became the beacon we sought."

Aditi nodded in agreement. "I remember wanting to do everything on my own – tie my shoes, choose my clothes, make my decisions."

Ramji smiled knowingly, "It's a natural progression. We crave autonomy and control. However, there's a twist in this journey. Once we achieve independence, we realize that there are moments when we still feel helpless."

Rohan chimed in, "Absolutely. As much as we want to be self-sufficient, there are situations where we don't know something, and that lack of knowledge can make us feel vulnerable."

Ramji's eyes sparkled with understanding,

"Exactly, Rohan. Not knowing can make us feel exposed, like we're back to being that child who needs guidance. This is where our education system's emphasis on individual achievement can sometimes become a stumbling block."

Vishwa leaned forward, intrigued. "So, our pursuit of independence sometimes comes full circle. We yearn for autonomy, but then we hesitate to admit our ignorance."

Ramji nodded, "That's the paradox. The fear of being seen as 'dependent' or 'incompetent' can hinder our growth. We often think that independence means knowing everything."

In a moment of reflection, Vishwa remarked, "None of us can claim to know everything; our limitations define us." Intrigued, he added, "I've heard whispers about a transformative framework you've designed. Can you provide us with a sneak peek?"

"Absolutely, Vishwa! Let me unveil 'The 7G Transcendental Framework,' a masterpiece I've intricately fashioned. Brace yourself, as this isn't just another course; it's a transformative odyssey. Envision a professional realm where you boldly navigate challenges, seize growth with unwavering confidence, and shatter barriers that stifle your boundless potential."

A sense of curiosity hung in the air as Ramji continued, "This framework isn't a mere set of guidelines; it's my brainchild designed to liberate ourselves from the confines of judgment. In the realm of professional development, it transcends mere skill acquisition, cultivating a mindset firmly anchored in the bedrock of psychological safety."

The room, once absorbed in the paradox of independence, now buzzed with the anticipation of a new journey – a journey into the depths of the 7G Transcendental Framework, where limitations dissolve, and the true potential of each individual emerges.

Vishwa's eyes lit up with curiosity, "The 7G Transcendental Framework sounds like the enchanted tool every professional yearns for! We're definitely eager for a live encounter with it. Also, the notion of Psychological Safety has piqued my interest. Could you delve deeper into that?"

Ramji nodded with conviction, "Absolutely. In the realm of a learning organization, psychological safety forms the very foundation where collaboration and growth flourish. Knowing that we won't face judgment for our lack of knowledge empowers us to embrace curiosity, venture into the unknown, and openly acknowledge our vulnerabilities."

Aakash added, "So, it's not about erasing our independence. It's about realizing that interdependence doesn't weaken us; it strengthens us."

"Certainly," stressed Ramji. "Embracing interdependence means recognizing that we're integral parts of a larger ecosystem. Just as a forest thrives on the collaboration of its inhabitants, our organization flourishes when departments work in perfect harmony."

Ramji's smile was reassuring, "That's the transformational journey we're on. When an organization creates an environment of psychological safety – where opinions are respected, and vulnerability is celebrated – individuals begin to shed their inhibitions. When you feel secure expressing your ideas, that's when innovation, creativity, and true growth take centre stage."

"You know,", "there's a story from my past that's always stayed with me, something that taught me a powerful lesson about how interconnectedness works in nature."

His team members leaned forward, eager to hear more. "It all began with a small seed my father gave me," Ramji continued, a smile touching his lips. "I planted it in a garden and watched it grow into a little plant. It was a thrilling experience, and I felt like I was solely responsible for its growth."

The team nodded, engrossed in the story. "But then, my father came over one day while I was tending to the plant," Ramji continued. "He looked at it and smiled, and that's when he dropped a truth bomb on me – a lesson about how plants are connected in ways we can't always see."

Ramji's voice, a storyteller weaving a tale of nature's secrets, resonated with a reflective cadence as he unraveled the wisdom passed down by his father. "It wasn't just my care that fueled my plant's growth," he mused. "It's as if there's a symphony at play, an orchestra of elements choreographing a botanical ballet. Sunlight, air, water, ether – each note harmonizing for the collective growth of not just one, but all the plants in this vibrant ecosystem."

The team, caught in the enchantment of Ramji's narrative, exchanged curious glances, their intrigue piqued. He went on to unveil the clandestine world beneath the soil, where plants communicate through an intricate network, sharing not just soil and water but also mutual support. "Think of it as their own community," Ramji elucidated, drawing parallels to human cooperation.

With a surge in enthusiasm, Ramji continued to paint the vivid picture of this hidden alliance. "Envision a plant, its roots delving deep for nutrients others might miss. These benevolent plants emit signals, an invitation of sorts. Nearby plants, attuned to the call, extend their roots toward the nutrient-rich source. It's akin to a neighborhood where resources are shared for the greater good."

As the team nodded in comprehension, Ramji seamlessly wove the water narrative into his botanical saga. "When it comes to water, the drama unfolds similarly," he elaborated. "Plants with deeper roots act as water conduits, drawing it from lower depths and generously redistributing it upwards. It's like a contractual agreement among neighbor, a communal effort where every plant benefits from the upward flow of this life-giving resource."

In that moment, the team not only saw the office as a workspace but as a thriving ecosystem, where each member, like the interconnected plants, played a vital role in the symphony of growth and collaboration.

A sense of realization dawned on the faces of his team members. "But that's not all," Ramji continued with enthusiasm. "The roots of different plants can physically intertwine, creating a connection for the exchange of water, nutrients, and more. It's like they're shaking hands underground. And when plants grow near each other, they grow quicker and healthier due to these interconnections. The same principle applies to humans; researchers have found that the longest-lived healthy adults had close friends, and this social connection may be a key factor contributing to their longevity."

Ramji's story was beginning to paint a vivid picture of the interconnected world beneath the surface. "And just like friends who look out for each other, some plants provide shade and protection," he added. "They create a shield against harsh elements, helping the smaller, more delicate plants thrive."

Ramji held a momentary pause, his face adorned with a gentle smile. "You grasp the essence of that lesson on interconnectedness – it transcended mere plants. It unveiled nature's artistry, weaving an elaborate tapestry of collaboration. It extends beyond flora – encompassing people, communities, and the vast expanse of our world. Like those plants, we're threads in a grander fabric, where our deeds and connections carry weight. It's a lesson etched in my heart since that enlightening moment."

As Ramji's story about the interconnectedness of plants settled within the minds of his team members, they each found themselves reflecting on their own experiences and drawing valuable insights. The conference room was filled with a tangible sense of resonance as they shared their thoughts.

Aditi, with a contemplative expression, spoke first. "Ramji's story reminded me of the times when I hesitated to ask for help because I didn't want to appear weak. Just like those plants supporting each other, it's important for us to lean on each other's strengths. We can't be experts in everything, and by acknowledging that, we can build a more collaborative and effective team."

Rohan chimed in, his voice filled with enthusiasm. "Absolutely! It made me think of our projects and how often we work in silos. Just like those plants sharing resources, we can achieve so much more when we openly share our knowledge and insights. Collaboration isn't about losing individuality; it's about creating something stronger together."

Aakash nodded, his eyes lit up with newfound realization. "Ramji's story hit home for me because I've sometimes hesitated to admit when I didn't know something. But just like those plants reaching out for nutrients, it's okay to seek knowledge from others. We have this incredible pool of expertise within our team, and tapping into it can lead to growth and innovation."

Vishwa leaned back, lost in thought. "The idea of roots physically intertwining struck me as a powerful symbol of connection. We might have different roles and responsibilities, but like those plants, we're all intertwined in our pursuit of a common goal. Supporting each other, sharing resources, and creating a network of support can only strengthen our collective efforts."

Aditi added to Vishwa's point, "And just like how some trees provide shade and protection to weaker plants and trees, we can offer mentorship and guidance to those who might need it. It's not about superiority; it's about nurturing growth. By embracing interdependence, we create an environment where learning is celebrated, and everyone can thrive."

Rohan shared his personal take on the lesson. "For me, the story underscored that it's okay to be vulnerable. Vulnerability doesn't weaken us; it strengthens our connections. Much like those plants responding to signals, our willingness to be open about our challenges and uncertainties can lead to shared growth and solutions."

As the team members continued to discuss the insights they had gained from Ramji's story, it became evident that the concept of interdependence had taken root in their minds. The metaphor of the interconnected plant network had provided them with a tangible representation of the power of collaboration and support.

Ramji sat back, quietly observing the exchange with a sense of satisfaction. He had hoped that sharing his story would ignite a spark of understanding about the importance of interdependence and psychological safety within their team. Seeing his team members engaged in such a meaningful dialogue affirmed his belief in the potential for growth and transformation that lay ahead.

As the session came to a close, Ramji invited the team to carry this newfound awareness with them into their daily interactions. He encouraged them to embrace the paradox of interdependence, recognizing that true strength comes not from isolation, but from the willingness to learn, share, and support one another. And with that, the team left the conference room, each member carrying a piece of the story with them, ready to weave it into their collective journey of growth and collaboration.

Takeaways

> **Independence vs. Interdependence:** *Understanding the paradox of independence and its impact on personal and professional growth.*

> *Realizing the cyclical nature of the pursuit of autonomy and its influence on vulnerability.*

> **Psychological Safety:** *Recognizing the foundational role of psychological safety in a learning organization.*

> *Empowering individuals to embrace curiosity, acknowledge vulnerabilities, and venture into the unknown.*

> **Interconnectedness and Collaboration:** *Drawing parallels between nature's interconnectedness and human collaboration.*

> *Understanding the significance of collaboration, shared resources, and mutual support in fostering growth.*

> **Nature's Lessons on Interconnectedness:** *Insight into the underground network of plant roots, emphasizing the exchange of resources.*

> *Realizing the parallels between plants' collaboration and human connections in communities and organizations.*

Attainments

> **Engagement and Curiosity:** *Capturing the team's interest and curiosity through a thought-provoking exploration.*

> *Creating an engaging environment that transitioned from the paradox of independence to the anticipation of a transformative journey.*

> **Introduction of 7G Framework:** *Unveiling a unique and comprehensive professional development framework.*

> *Positioning the 7G Transcendental Framework as a tool for navigating challenges and unlocking boundless potential.*

- ➢ **Understanding Psychological Safety:** *Facilitating a deeper understanding of psychological safety and its role in organizational growth.*

  Encouraging open dialogue and reflections on the team's experiences and challenges.

- ➢ **Nature's Metaphor for Collaboration:** *Employing a powerful metaphor of interconnected plants to illustrate collaboration.*

  Successfully conveying the importance of interdependence and mutual support within the team.

- ➢ **Team Reflection and Insight Sharing:** *Orchestrating a reflective session where team members openly shared insights.*

  Fostering a sense of realization and resonance among team members regarding their roles in the organizational ecosystem.

- ➢ **Encouraging Vulnerability and Growth:** *Promoting the acceptance of vulnerability as a strength.*

  Inspiring a commitment to openness about challenges, uncertainties, and the collective pursuit of growth.

- ➢ **Igniting a Spark for Growth and Transformation:** *Sparking a meaningful dialogue that affirmed the team's potential for growth and transformation.*

  Encouraging team members to carry the newfound awareness of interdependence into their daily interactions.

Applying the Dynamic 7G Transcendental Framework

Growth:

Introducing the 7G Transcendental Framework as a tool for bold navigation of challenges and seizing growth with confidence.

Encouraging the team to envision a professional realm where limitations dissolve, and individual potential emerges.

Guidance:

Referring to Stephen Covey's principle, emphasizing the need for independence before interdependence.

Guiding the team through the exploration of collaboration's depth and intricacies.

Grit:

Acknowledging the paradox of independence, highlighting the team's burning desire for autonomy.

Addressing the vulnerability that accompanies independence, emphasizing the need for resilience and perseverance.

Gallantry:

Sharing a personal story about interconnectedness in nature, showcasing gallantry in understanding and appreciating the collaborative dynamics.

Painting a vivid picture of the hidden alliances in the plant world, portraying a sense of wonder and gallantry in acknowledging the intricacies of nature.

Gratitude:

Expressing gratitude for the team's engagement and curiosity in response to the unveiling of the 7G Transcendental Framework.

Appreciating the team's openness in reflecting on personal experiences and drawing valuable insights.

Glow:

Introducing the concept of psychological safety as a foundational element in the learning organization.

Emphasizing that psychological safety allows for the glow of innovation, creativity, and true growth within the team.

Greatness:

Inspiring greatness by illustrating the interconnectedness of individuals, communities, and the world.

Encouraging the team to embrace interdependence, recognizing that true strength comes from learning, sharing, and supporting one another.

"Within the crucible of challenges, where adversity casts its shadow, unfolds the profound artistry of transformation. Transcendental professionals don't just weather storms; they dance in the rain of difficulties, weaving setbacks into an opportunity tapestry. May collective resilience reshape adversity into the fertile ground from which extraordinary opportunities bloom, forging a legacy of triumph for the shared journey ahead."

Episode #4:

Bridging Shadows: A Pact with the Unknown

The sun cast a gentle glow over the office, painting a tranquil scene that belied the storm about to hit. Colleagues exchanged morning greetings, and the aroma of freshly brewed coffee lingered in the air. The hum of computers filled the workspace with a soothing rhythm. It was a calm day, much like any other, until the screens flickered with an ominous message.

Aditi's heart raced as she stared at the ominous message on her screen: "Your Systems Have Been Compromised." The words seemed etched into her mind, refusing to fade away like a fleeting illusion. A sense of unease spread through her, and she instinctively glanced around, wondering if her colleagues were experiencing the same unsettling sight.

As if in a cruel twist of fate, her gaze met Rohan's worried eyes from across the room. He mouthed the words, "You too?" and Aditi could only nod, the weight of the situation sinking in. A quick survey of her surroundings revealed a similar scene unfolding across the office. Colleagues sat frozen at their desks, their screens displaying the same chilling message.

A hushed murmur of disbelief began to circulate, growing in intensity like a distant storm gathering momentum. The sense of panic was tangible, rippling through the office like a shock-wave. It was as if a shadow had suddenly descended upon the once-bustling workspace, casting doubt and uncertainty over their daily routines.

Whispers turned into urgent conversations as employees exchanged worried glances and hastily exchanged theories. The pop-up was now a common thread that tied everyone together, their individual experiences woven into a shared narrative of concern. Phones buzzed with messages, and the low hum of distress filled the air.

Rohan's brow furrowed as he read the message in all other systems. "What the...? Is this some kind of prank?"

Aditi shook her head, her heart beginning to race. "I don't think so. This looks serious."

As if on cue, an almost synchronized chorus of gasps and exclamations rippled through the office. The unsettling message had spread like wildfire, appearing on screens all around the room.

Vishwa, the CEO, was among the first to react. He rushed out of his office and into the midst of the chaos, his authoritative presence attempting to quell the rising panic.

"Everyone, calm down," he said, his voice firm but reassuring. "We're looking into this. We'll get to the bottom of it."

The chaos in the office began to subside, but the tension remained perceptible. Vishwa called for a meeting of the IT Security Team and the Heads of Departments in the conference room.

In the conference room, the atmosphere was charged with anxiety and uncertainty. The teams filled the seats, their faces reflecting a mix of confusion and concern.

Vishwa stepped in front of the room, his presence commanding attention. "I know you're all worried about the message that appeared on our screens. We take this seriously, and we're already investigating the situation."

Sourav, the Head of IT Security, raised his hand. "We've identified that our systems have indeed been compromised," he said, his voice resolute. "We're working to understand the extent of the breach."

Vishwa's eyes scanned the room with urgency. "Time is of the essence. Sourav, gather your team swiftly and dig deep into this. We can't afford to overlook this breach; it demands our immediate attention."

In the midst of this turmoil, Sourav's mind landed on Ramji, a name that resonated with whispers of miraculous salvation. He recalled stories of how Ramji had repeatedly emerged as the beacon of hope, the mastermind behind ingenious solutions when all seemed hopelessly lost. In this dire hour, Sourav knew that he had to make the call. The fate of their security and their team's morale hung in the balance, and they needed Ramji's expertise to tip the scales in their favor.

Sourav nodded. "Understood." As everyone left the conference room, Aditi approached Sourav. "This is serious, Sourav. We can't let our systems stay vulnerable like this."

In the next harrowing hours, the IT Security team toiled ceaselessly in the face of an insidious threat. They explored the intricate logs in detail, desperately attempting to trace the breach that had pierced their digital fortress. Frustration and despair loomed like ominous shadows as the full extent of the malevolent intrusion became chillingly apparent.

As each moment unfolded, the gravity of their mission pressed down on them. Despite temporarily halting the onslaught, the patch they applied felt like a delicate bandage on a gaping wound—a fragile defense restraining the unyielding storm. This interim relief was desperate and precarious, with a keen awareness that the storm was far from subsiding. The hacker's unyielding cunning and the multitude of vulnerabilities hidden within their systems remained persistent threats, poised to plunge them back into the depths of digital chaos.

The room hung heavy with tension, a palpable anxiety that gripped every team member. Exhausted from tireless efforts to fortify their systems against an overwhelming threat, the team faced not just a challenge but stood on the edge of potential disaster. As Sourav paced, the gravity of the moment loomed ominously. A breakthrough wasn't just a wish; it was a vital lifeline they urgently needed. Sourav was convinced – the situation demanded the expertise of a seasoned crisis management professional.

Sourav rang Ramji

Sourav: Ramji, I'm relieved to reach out to you. We're dealing with a big security breach, and we've patched it up temporarily. But we're worried about the long-term impact. We need your help to figure out what to do next.

Ramji: I'm here to listen, Sourav. Please go ahead and tell me about the situation.

Sourav: Well, you see, it's like this – our security systems have been compromised. It's a massive breach, and we're scrambling to contain the damage and fix the vulnerabilities.

Ramji: I can sense the urgency in your voice, Sourav. Breaches can indeed be challenging to handle. Can you provide me with more details about the nature of the breach and how your team is approaching it?

Sourav: Of course. We've been analyzing the data logs and trying to identify the hacker's entry point. It's been a constant back-and-forth, but we're having a hard time tracing the breach back to its origin.

Ramji: It sounds like you're dealing with a situation that requires careful navigation. It reminds me of tending to a garden. Sourav: (curiously) A garden? How so?

Ramji: "Envision your IT landscape as a garden, disrupted by a security breach, akin to an invasive weed. To restore harmony, just as a gardener studies soil conditions, plant growth, and factors leading to weed infestations, your team must explore the digital landscape for the root cause.

Sourav: (intrigued) So, you're saying we need to understand the environment in which the breach occurred?

Ramji: Precisely. Much like a gardener would analyze the soil, the sun exposure, and the surrounding ecosystem, your team should scrutinize the digital environment where the breach happened. Look for patterns, anomalies, and any vulnerabilities that might have been exploited. Introduce an holistic approach.

Sourav: (thoughtful) That's an interesting perspective. It's a bit like conducting a security audit, but instead of just checking for known issues, we need to dive deeper, like identifying where the soil might be eroding and how pests could be infiltrating the system.

Ramji: You've got it, Sourav. It's about understanding the whole ecosystem, not just the obvious threats. This holistic approach can reveal unexpected weaknesses and help prevent future breaches.

Sourav: Thanks, Ramji. I'll gather the team and start our "gardening" process right away.

Ramji: Excellent. Remember, it's not just about removing the weeds but ensuring the soil becomes inhospitable to them in the first place. Just as a weed can be a symptom of an underlying issue in a garden, a breach might be indicative of vulnerabilities in your security measures. By tracing the breach's path, you might uncover weaknesses that need strengthening.

Sourav's mind was immediately engaged. "Yes, that's what it feels like – an invasive weed that's disrupting the harmony of our system."

"Absolutely," Ramji added. "Observe the growth pattern as it traces back to its origin. They track the 'weeds' to uncover their source."

Sourav's perspective was shifting. "So, you're saying we should trace the hacker's entry points back to the source – the root of the breach?

"Yes," Ramji said, "think of these entry points as the pathways these 'weeds' take to infiltrate our space. By understanding their path, you can find the root cause and eliminate it."

Sourav: I'll definitely keep that in mind. Thanks again, Ramji. Your guidance means a lot.

Ramji smiled warmly at Sourav's gratitude. "You're welcome, Sourav. Keep me updated on your progress. And remember, just as a skilled gardener turns challenges into opportunities, you can do the same with this situation.

Think of it like this, a seed uses both sunlight and darkness to grow, and in our case, this crisis, as unsettling as it is, can be the darkness that fosters our growth." Sourav, though still uncertain about the seed analogy, thanked Ramji for his unwavering support.

Ramji: Always here to help. Take care, Sourav.

Sourav immediately addressed the team, "Listen, everyone," he began. "We're dealing with a digital garden here, and just like a skilled gardener, we need to follow the growth of these 'weeds' to find the root. Think of these entry points as the pathways these 'weeds' take to infiltrate our space."

Ankita, a member of the team, raised her hand. "But how do we do that? It's like trying to find a single weed in a vast garden."

Sourav smiled, inspired by the analogy. "You're right, Ankita. But remember, gardeners often use indicators – patterns, footprints, and even visual cues – to identify where the weeds are most likely to emerge. Our systems leave traces, just like footprints in a garden. If we follow these digital 'footprints,' we might just find the entry point."

His words ignited a renewed determination in the team. They began to explore the logs and data once again, this time with a focused approach – tracing the pathways of the hacker's entry, just as gardeners might follow the growth patterns of weeds.

Hours turned into a methodical pursuit. The team examined the data, identified patterns, and started connecting the dots. Just like skilled gardeners can anticipate the emergence of weeds based on soil conditions, the IT Security team started anticipating the hacker's moves based on the digital landscape.

And then, finally, it happened. The team identified an anomaly in the logs – a slight deviation from the usual pattern. Like a gardener discovering a misshapen growth among healthy plants, they had found a sign of the hacker's presence.

Sourav's excitement was palpable. "We've got it!" he exclaimed. "This is the pathway they used."

As they delved deeper into the anomaly, they began to unravel the hacker's techniques. They were following the path back to the root and then closed the breach, just as Ramji's analogy had guided them. The company's systems were up and the Team heaved a huge sigh of relief.

Sourav then summoned a meeting with the Leadership team with a proposal "I know this might sound unconventional," Sourav began, his voice steady despite the skeptical glances around the room. "But think about it. This hacker has managed to breach our security. They're skilled, and they have a motive. Instead of just shutting them out and reporting them, what if we engaged with them?"

The room fell into a stunned silence. Vishwa leaned forward, intrigued by Sourav's proposal. "Engage with them? What do you mean?"

Sourav met Vishwa's gaze, his resolve unwavering. "I mean reaching out to the hacker, talking to them, and understanding their perspective. If we can get into their mind, we can anticipate their moves better. We can identify vulnerabilities before they do."

A murmur of uncertainty rippled through the room, but Sourav continued, his voice gaining momentum. "Think about it. Every crisis is an opportunity. This hacker has exposed a weakness in our armour. Instead of just fixing it and moving on, what if we used their expertise to strengthen our defence?"

Sourav's words hung in the air, daring the team to embrace the unorthodox approach. Slowly, Vishwa nodded. "It's a risk, Sourav, but it's a calculated risk. If we can truly turn this situation around, it might just change the game for us."

With Vishwa firmly in his corner, Sourav fearlessly reached out to the hacker. Utilizing secure channels, he initiated a text conversation, extending a genuine interest in comprehending the hacker's motivations and insights. While initially cautious, the hacker soon became intrigued by the unexpected overture and willingly shared his contact number.

Sourav: [Dialing the number]

Hacker: [Answering the call] Hello?

Sourav: Hi, this is Sourav. I appreciate you taking my call.

Hacker: Yeah, I've been thinking about what you said in your messages. It's intriguing, I'll admit.

Sourav: I'm glad to hear that. I believe we can turn this situation into something positive.

Hacker: As the hacker's fingers moved with practiced precision, there was a hint of pride in his voice, a subtle arrogance that came from mastering the digital realm.

"You see," he remarked, "hacking, it's an art. It's about understanding the intricate dance of code, exploiting the weaknesses, and taking control. It's not just about the money, although that's a nice bonus. It's about outsmarting the system, showing that nothing is impenetrable. But, you know, sometimes, late at night, I wonder if I've crossed a line, if I've let my talents serve the wrong purpose. There's a price to pay for this knowledge, a weight that lingers even in the realm of ones and zeros.".

Sourav: I understand your concern. What I'm proposing is a different path. We want to work with you to strengthen our security.

Hacker: And why should I trust you?

Sourav: Trust is a two-way street. We both have something to gain here. Your skills can make our systems better protected, and you'll be recognized for it.

Hacker: You really think your company would hire someone like me?

Sourav: We believe in giving people second chances. We're looking at the bigger picture here - making sure our platform is secure for millions of users.

Hacker: And what do I get out of this, other than not being hunted down?

Sourav: You'll be acknowledged for your contributions, and we'll work out a compensation package that reflects your expertise and threw a compensation range.

Hacker: It's an enticing proposition, but what assurance do I have that you're not attempting to track me down?

Sourav: Rest assured, this is a bonafide opportunity. We're seeking a new outlook to enhance our security measures, and there won't be any tracking involved.

Hacker: Alright, let's say I'm in. What's the next step?

Sourav: We'll start by setting up a secure channel of communication. We can discuss the details and come up with a plan to identify vulnerabilities. I'm also texting you the tentative compensation approved by our management.

Hacker: Sure, but I'll need some time to think it over. This is a big decision.

Sourav: Take all the time you need. Just remember, this is a chance to use your skills for a positive impact and I am not reporting you till you come back with your decision and a token of trust.

Hacker: I'll be in touch soon.

Sourav: Looking forward to it. I would like to meet you in our office. Let's make the digital world safer together.

Weeks passed since Sourav's initial conversation with the hacker. The tension in the office had evolved into a sense of anticipation, curiosity, and cautious hope. Aditi, Rohan, and the entire team had become accustomed to the unorthodox approach that Sourav had championed. Finally, the hacker responded that he was willing to meet.

The meeting room was set up meticulously. Vishwa, Aditi, Rohan, and the rest of the team gathered, their expressions a mix of uncertainty and curiosity. Sourav, the mastermind behind this audacious plan, stood at the front of the room, his confidence unwavering.

Vishwa glanced around the room before turning his attention to Sourav. "This is a bold move, Sourav. Are you sure about this?"

Sourav nodded, his eyes determined. "You're spot on, Vishwa. This crisis is a chance for us to transform it into an advantage," Sourav affirmed. Continuing, he explained, "With multiple persona logins worldwide, our Virtual Gaming Platform presents vast opportunities for hackers. To secure our platform, we need to take these essential steps."

As the room buzzed with anticipation, the door opened, and the hacker walked in – a figure cloaked in mystery, their identity hidden behind a digital alias. The tension in the room was palpable as everyone locked their eyes on the figure who had once been their adversary.

Sourav stepped forward, extending his hand in a gesture of goodwill. "Thank you for being here."

The hacker, dressed in casual attire, shook Sourav's hand with a hint of a smile. "You have a convincing way of making a point, Sourav."

Sourav returned the smile. "I believe in turning challenges into opportunities. That's what this meeting is about."

Vishwa leaned forward, intrigued by the situation. "So, how do you propose we work together?"

The hacker's eyes scanned the room before settling on Sourav. "I've done my research. I know what your platform is about, and I know the vulnerabilities that exist. I can help you plug those gaps, make your system more secure."

Aditi couldn't help but interject. "And what's in it for you?" The hacker's expression turned serious. "Recognition, for one. The chance to prove that I can use my skills for something positive. Plus, the compensation you offered isn't bad either."

Rohan leaned forward. "But how can we trust you? You've breached our security before."

The hacker's gaze met Rohan's, earnestness in their eyes. "True, I breached your security. But that was a test. A way to show you that there were vulnerabilities. Think of it as a wake-up call."

Sourav nodded. "We've been blinded by our own successes. We thought we were impenetrable. But you showed us otherwise."

The hacker's voice softened. "I'm not your enemy, despite how it may seem. I saw an opportunity, and I took it. Now, I see another opportunity – to use my skills to strengthen your security."

Vishwa leaned back in his chair, considering the proposal. "This is unconventional, to say the least. But in a rapidly changing digital landscape, unconventional might just be what we need."

Sourav turned to the hacker. "If we go ahead with this, it won't be easy. You'll have to earn our trust."

The hacker nodded. "I understand. I'm willing to prove myself."

Vishwa looked around the room, a mixture of determination and pragmatism in his eyes. "Then it's settled. We'll engage you as a consultant, provided you adhere to strict guidelines and follow our rules."

The hacker extended his hand once again. "Deal."

As the handshake sealed the agreement, the room was filled with a sense of cautious optimism. The hacker, once a nameless adversary, had become an unexpected ally in their quest for digital security.

The official on-boarding formalities were completed. Weeks turned into months, and the hacker, now known by his real name, Mark, worked alongside the IT Security team. He meticulously identified vulnerabilities, suggested improvements, and helped strengthen the platform's defense.

The transformation was undeniable. The once-shaky security infrastructure had evolved into a fortress, thanks to the collaboration between the company and Mark. The digital garden that had once been riddled with 'weeds' was now thriving with resilience.

Saurav often found himself reflecting on the wisdom Ramji had shared: "A seed uses both light and darkness to grow." This simple yet profound analogy had a profound impact on him.

The crisis, the breach that had cast a shadow over their operations, had indeed been the darkness. However, it was Ramji's guidance and the lessons learned from that challenging period that had served as the guiding light, illuminating the path to growth and improvement. In time, they realized that this breach, as unsettling as it was, had become the catalyst for their organization's transformation, making them stronger and more resilient in the face of future challenges.

The company's security measures became a benchmark, setting an example for others in the industry. The unconventional partnership between Sourav, the IT Security team, and Mark served as a testament to the power of turning adversity into opportunity.

Indeed, as time went on, the lesson from Ramji's garden analogy continued to resonate in the IT Security Department. It was clear that just as a skilled gardener knows when to seek expertise from others, Cognos needed a trusted third-party partner with specialized knowledge in IT security to strengthen its defense.

Ramji consistently emphasized the importance of bringing in this expert third party whenever their internal expertise fell short.

Whether it was for consulting, workshops, or specialized solutions, the idea of engaging with these vendors became a cornerstone of their security strategy. Ramji's wisdom had set the seeds of a proactive approach to IT security that would, with time, grow into a robust and resilient ecosystem.

As the IT Security team adapted to their evolving roles and responsibilities, they couldn't help but feel a sense of achievement. But little did they know, a storm was brewing on the horizon – a storm that would challenge their newfound principles and camaraderie to the core.

One crisp morning, precisely a fortnight into Mark's tenure with the company, Vishwa urgently summoned the team for an impromptu meeting. The typically serene and collected CEO wore a rare expression of concern, his brow furrowed as he addressed the assembled team. "I must share with you all that we find ourselves in the midst of a crisis."

Takeaways

- **Holistic Approach to Security:** *Holistic approach to security, likening it to a gardener analyzing the entire ecosystem.*

  Emphasized the need to understand the digital environment, scrutinize patterns, anomalies, and vulnerabilities.

- **Digital Gardening Analogy:** *Analogy of a gardener, guiding Sourav to view the breach as an invasive weed disrupting the system.*

  Traced the hacker's entry points back to the source, similar to identifying the root cause in a garden.

- **Understanding the Ecosystem:** *Advised Sourav to understand the entire digital ecosystem, not just obvious threats.*

This approach could reveal unexpected weaknesses, aiding in preventing future breaches.

➤ **Turning Challenges into Opportunities:** *Perspective shift, seeing the crisis as an opportunity.*

Instead of solely fixing the breach, they engaged with the hacker to turn the situation into a positive transformation for the company.

Attainments

➤ **Perspective Shift:** *Facilitated a paradigm shift in the team's perspective towards cybersecurity.*

Introduced a groundbreaking approach inspired by the garden analogy, encouraging the team to view their digital landscape as a garden in need of careful cultivation.

➤ **Holistic Mindset:** *Provided crucial guidance on embracing a holistic mindset in approaching cybersecurity challenges.*

Emphasized the importance of understanding the entire digital ecosystem, akin to a gardener analyzing the soil, sun exposure, and the surrounding environment.

➤ **Path Tracing:** *Played a pivotal role in guiding the IT Security team's response to the breach.*

Encouraged the team to trace the hacker's pathways meticulously, focusing on identifying the root cause of the breach rather than just addressing the surface issues.

➤ **Empowerment of Sourav:** *Empowered Sourav to seek external expertise during a critical situation.*

Sourav reached out for expert advice, showcasing the importance of seeking guidance from external sources, especially in high-stakes scenarios.

> **Foundational Principle:** *The garden analogy became a foundational principle for the organization's cybersecurity strategy.*

Set the seeds for a proactive approach to IT security, becoming a guiding principle for the team's future endeavors.

> **Unconventional Partnership:** *Led to an unconventional but successful partnership with the hacker, Mark.*

Instead of viewing Mark as a threat, the approach turned him into an asset for cybersecurity, showcasing the transformative power of innovative thinking.

> **Benchmark in Security:** *The company's security measures, influenced by teachings, became an industry benchmark.*

The success of the collaborative approach, especially the partnership with Mark, showcased the effectiveness of embracing unconventional strategies in cybersecurity.

Applying the Dynamic 7G Transcendental Framework

Growth:

Sourav's unconventional approach, driven by the 7G Transcendental Framework, led to significant growth in the company's security measures.

The crisis became a catalyst for organizational transformation and resilience.

Guidance:

Provided guidance on a holistic security approach and the analogy of the digital garden, aligning with the principles of the 7G Framework.

Sourav, in turn, provided guidance to the team, steering them towards engaging with the hacker for a positive outcome.

Grit:

The IT Security team, under Sourav's leadership, displayed determination in fortifying the system against the breach.

The unconventional decision to engage with the hacker also demonstrated courage and determination.

Gallantry:

Sourav's proposal to engage with the hacker, even in the face of skepticism, showcased gallantry.

It was a bold move to turn a potential adversary into an ally for the greater good.

Gratitude:

Sourav expressed gratitude towards guidance for their contribution.

The company offered the hacker recognition and compensation, expressing gratitude for his skills.

Glow:

The collaboration with the hacker, Mark, brought a positive glow to the company's security measures.

The successful partnership illuminated a path of growth and improvement.

Greatness:

The unconventional collaboration led by Sourav, demonstrated greatness by setting a benchmark in security measures.

The company's approach became an example for the industry, showcasing greatness in turning adversity into an opportunity.

"In the crucible of challenges, emerges The Resilient Alliance—an emotional bond that endures amidst adversity. As leaders, commitment transcends mere prosperity; it's a profound vow to traverse hardship collectively. Within the shared symphony of resilience, harmonies resound, echoing an unwavering dedication to surmount every trial as a united force."

Episode #5:

Harmony in Crisis: Nurturing Growth Through Unlikely Alliances

The meeting room crackled with a palpable tension, each breath seemingly heavy with the weight of the impending crisis. Vishwa, the charismatic CEO of Cognos, stood resolute at the head of the room, his usually affable demeanor replaced with a gravity that captured the room's attention. The faces of the team members, a mixture of concern and determination, were lit by the glow of the presentation screen, which displayed the reality of their situation.

Vishwa's eyes, usually alight with optimism, swept his gaze across the room, connecting with the eyes of each team member. His look conveyed a resolute determination, a silent plea to unite in the face of the impending storm. "Ladies and gentlemen," he declared, his voice blending both solemnity and defiance, "the supply chain disruption of VR chips amid the ongoing crisis has thrown a challenging shadow over our carefully crafted plans. Our journey, filled with countless hours of unwavering effort, now stands at a pivotal crossroads."

The words hung in the air, the weight of their significance noticeable. Aditi leaned slightly forward, her expressive eyes a mirror of the collective sentiment. "This setback threatens to redefine our path," she murmured, the weight of the words seeping into the hearts of her colleagues.

As if on cue, Ajay, the Head of Procurement, moved slightly, the click of his phone's keys punctuating the silence. The room's gaze shifted towards him as he stood up, his posture commanding attention. "Excuse me for a moment," he said, his tone carrying a sense of urgency and determination.

The room watched with a mix of curiosity and anticipation as Ajay navigated through his phone. A hushed silence enveloped them as he initiated a virtual call in Teams, his fingers moving swiftly yet purposefully.

A collective breath seemed to be held as the call connected, and Anil Kumar, the CEO of their current supplier's face appeared on the screen. The room's energy seemed to crystallize, the digital connection linking their fates.

Ajay's gaze locked onto the screen, his expression focused and unyielding. The air grew charged with a mixture of tension and anticipation, the glow from his computer screen casting sharp lines on his face, enhancing the determined set of his features.

"I've had enough," Ajay's voice was firm, unyielding. "The constant delays, it's unacceptable. We're at a critical juncture, and we can't afford any more setbacks."

Anil, on the other end of the call, shifted uncomfortably in his seat, his expression a mixture of concern and defensiveness. "Ajay, please understand that we're facing unprecedented challenges due to the crisis. Our entire raw material supply chain has been disrupted."

Ajay's gaze didn't waver, his tone unwavering. "I do understand the challenges, and that's precisely why we need partners who are committed to overcoming them. Our entire project hinges on the delivery of those VR chips. We can't proceed with uncertainty looming over us."

Anil's voice softened, an attempt to regain some ground. "Ajay, I assure you, we're working around the clock to resolve the issues."

Ajay's expression hardened further, his frustration palpable. "Actions speak louder than words. We've seen a pattern of promises.

Our patience is exhausted, and our vision demands partners who can rise to the occasion."

Anil's face tightened, realizing the gravity of the situation. "Ajay, please give us another chance. We can provide a timeline for resolution and compensate for the delays."

Ajay leaned forward, his eyes narrowing. "This isn't just about compensation. It's about the trust we placed in your company and the responsibility you took on. We're terminating our agreement."

There was a palpable silence in the room as the weight of Ajay's words settled in. Anil's complexion grew noticeably paler, and his eyes widened in sheer astonishment. "Ajay, I implore you to reconsider. Our partnership has proven mutually advantageous throughout, and this marks the inaugural project with VR chip prerequisites."

Ajay's tone remained resolute, unyielding. "Beneficial partnerships are built on reliability and trust. We need certainty now, not empty promises. Our team has worked tirelessly, and we can't afford any more uncertainty."

Anil's shoulders slumped, his voice a mix of frustration and resignation. "I understand. If this is the decision you've made, I can't stop you. But please know that we truly regret the situation."

Ajay responded, "We understand," the weight of his words echoing with a sense of understanding.

The call was disconnected

Vishwa and the team acknowledged Ajay's resolute decisions, though Vishwa seemed worried. They understood that these steps were crucial in maintaining their vision and commitment to excellence.

"I have reached out to three suppliers," Ajay announced, his voice carrying an air of determination. "And we will get the best quote. We've set up a competition among them, each vying to provide us with the most competitive offer." Ajay's focus was only on a quick turn around time and not on long term strategy, in this case.

The room buzzed with anticipation. Aditi leaned forward, her eyes gleaming with excitement. "It's a bold move, though not ideal, Ajay. Making them compete for our partnership will undoubtedly give us the upper hand."

Ajay nodded with a confident smile. "You got it, Aditi. This shows them we're serious, aiming not just for the best price but their genuine commitment. Yes, bringing in a new vendor adds uncertainty and takes time, but we need to make a swift decision."

Just as the team's determination and energy were building, they spotted a figure in the hallway through the glass door of the conference room. It was Ramji, the Transcendental Professional and expert who had arrived to discuss consulting assignments and workshop plans with Vishwa.

Vishwa's face brightened with excitement. "Ramji is here! Let's welcome him inside, even though his initial visit had a different agenda."

Aditi hurried to the door and extended a warm welcome. "Ramji, we're right in the middle of a strategy session, discussing how to navigate the procurement crisis. Your insights could be invaluable to us."

Ramji smiled, "Procurement crisis, you say? Sounds like a challenge that demands a creative approach. I'd be honored to join you."

Ramji entered the room, a sense of excitement spread among the team members. His reputation as a problem solver and an innovative thinker was well-known, and his presence brought a renewed sense of purpose to the meeting.

"Ramji," Ajay called out, his voice carrying a note of warmth that contrasted with the tension in the room. "We're thrilled to have you here."

Ramji, momentarily surprised by the invitation, quickly made his way to the table. With a genuine smile, Ajay extended his hand in a gesture of camaraderie. "Ajay, The Head of Procurement, in light of recent developments, I believe your insights could be invaluable."

Ramji's grip was firm, his expression a blend of curiosity and readiness. "Thank you, Ajay. I appreciate the inclusion."

Ajay's eyes met Ramji's, and he delved into the chain of events that unfolded, culminating in the recent decision to terminate the supplier just moments ago

Ramji nodded, absorbing the gravity of the situation.

"We wish to seek your input to the current situation, Ramji," Vishwa says.

Ramji responded, his voice measured and deliberate, "Before we proceed, have we explored why our current supplier missed the deadline? Have we tried to understand the situation from their end? As Stephen Covey said, *'Seek to understand first, before trying to be understood.'*"

Ajay's brow furrowed slightly, the question prompting a moment of reflection. "You raised a valid point, Ramji. We've been focused on our end, but understanding their challenges could indeed provide valuable insights."

Ramji's gaze shifted from Ajay to the entire team, his expression one of encouraging collaboration.

"Exactly. Partnerships are built on a foundation of mutual benefit. Before we make any decisions, let's ensure we have a clear understanding of the challenges they're facing. This can guide us in finding a solution that aligns with our vision and values."

He then took a breath and began to share an illustrative story. "Let me draw a parallel from the business world. Consider the case of two giants in the automotive industry, Ford and Toyota."

Ramji's voice held a mix of intrigue and wisdom as he continued…

"In the early 1980s, the automotive industry faced significant challenges, mirroring the struggles in various sectors due to economic downturns and shifting consumer preferences. Ford and Toyota, two industry giants, responded uniquely to these challenges, with far-reaching consequences.

Ford, guided by different CEOs, adopted a competitive stance with suppliers, driven by a cost-saving mentality and a focus on driving down prices. The company frequently changed suppliers to secure the lowest component prices, fostering cutthroat competition among them. While this approach provided short-term financial gains, it strained relationships and lacked long-term commitment between Ford and its suppliers.

In contrast, Toyota pursued an approach centered on collaboration, partnership, and shared growth. Viewing suppliers as essential partners, Toyota prioritized stable and reliable supplier relationships for consistent product quality, efficient production, and innovation. Instead of constantly seeking lower prices, Toyota worked closely with a smaller number of suppliers, investing time and resources in building lasting relationships.

One of Toyota's impactful practices was its commitment to helping suppliers enhance their processes and capabilities. Sharing knowledge, providing technical assistance, and extending financial support enabled suppliers to improve their efficiency and quality standards, fostering a culture of continuous improvement throughout the supply chain.

Toyota's approach proved crucial during challenging periods like the oil crisis of the 1970s and subsequent economic downturn. Their consistent investments in suppliers and collaborative ethos resulted in mutual growth and innovation, creating an integrated supply chain capable of adapting to market changes.

The culmination of these efforts became evident when Toyota surpassed Ford as the world's second-largest automaker, while Ford faced bankruptcy and sought government assistance. The principles of shared growth and partnership laid the foundation for Toyota's remarkable rise, highlighting the potency of nurturing long-term relationships over the short-term gains of competitive price negotiations.

The sharp contrast between Ford and Toyota serves as a powerful lesson for businesses across industries, emphasizing the importance of viewing suppliers as strategic partners rather than transactional entities. While Ford's cutthroat competition strategy yielded temporary gains, Toyota's commitment to collaboration and mutual growth propelled it to sustained success."

Ramji's words lingered in the room, creating an atmosphere charged with reflection and inspiration.

"In essence," Ramji began, his voice carrying a contemplative tone, "changing suppliers is akin to uprooting a plant in search of better soil. Just as we might believe altering the environment will resolve a plant's challenges, we may think that changing suppliers will solve our immediate issues. However, genuine growth requires more than change; it demands nurturing."

A deliberate pause allowed the imagery to settle before he continued. "Picture a garden. When we plant a seed, we don't expect it to flourish overnight. It necessitates time, effort, and consistent care for that seed to evolve into a thriving plant. Similarly, our supplier relationships need time to take root and develop."

Ramji's gaze traversed the room, his eyes conveying the depth of his analogy. "Much like a garden where plants thrive with nurturing, our partnerships can also flourish when we invest in understanding, collaboration, and mutual growth."

Another pause let his words linger before he delved deeper into the analogy. "Consider the role of sunlight and water in a garden. Sunlight provides energy, while water nourishes and sustains. In our partnerships, transparency and communication act as our 'sunlight' – they provide the energy and clarity necessary for growth. And just as water is vital for a plant's survival, trust and commitment are the 'water' that nurtures our partnerships."

Ramji's hands gestured gracefully, painting the analogy into reality. "In a garden, challenges arise – weather changes, pests, and disease. Yet, we don't uproot plants at the first sign of trouble. Instead, we work to understand the underlying issues and find solutions. Similarly, in our supplier relationships, understanding their challenges and collaborating for solutions is essential for long-term success."

He took a moment to let his words sink in before concluding with a powerful insight. "A garden doesn't thrive by constantly transplanting its plants. Likewise, our partnerships won't flourish if we keep shifting from supplier to supplier. Let's be the gardeners of our alliances, nurturing them with patience, trust, and a shared commitment to growth."

The room seemed to hold its breath, the weight of Ramji's analogy and the wisdom it carried filling the air. It served as a reminder that beneath the complexities of business, the principles of nature held valuable lessons. Their partnerships, much like a garden, possessed the potential to bloom into something truly remarkable when tended with care and intention.

With Ramji's analogy still resonating in the room, Ajay's determination to find a solution was reignited. Taking a deep breath, he asked permission to proceed with an immediate course correction. Vishwa, sensing the shift in Ajay's energy, nodded in agreement, signaling for him to continue.

"Ramji," Ajay began, "your analogy has shed light on the importance of understanding and nurturing our supplier relationships. Instead of hastily seeking new suppliers, let's take a step back and delve into the challenges our current supplier is facing. Understanding their perspective may reveal avenues for collaboration and solutions."

The room, now charged with a renewed sense of purpose, nodded in agreement. Ajay continued, "I propose that we engage in open and transparent communication with our current supplier. Let's express our concerns, listen to their challenges, and explore ways in which we can collectively overcome the hurdles we face."

Vishwa, fully aligned with the shift in strategy, added, "Ajay, you've demonstrated leadership by adapting the new approach. I believe this collaborative stance aligns with our values and long-term vision. It's not just about solving the immediate crisis but building relationships that withstand the test of time."

Ajay, empowered by the support, began outlining a plan. "I'll schedule a meeting with our current supplier immediately. We'll approach this with empathy, seeking to understand their challenges and, in turn, communicating our expectations and commitments. It's time to water our garden, as Ramji would say."

Aditi, keenly observing the developing situation, suggested, "Let's bring in key stakeholders from both sides. Collaborating in this way ensures a thorough grasp of the situation, building trust and laying the foundation for impactful solutions."

The team, now fully engaged in the course correction, started brainstorming on the key stakeholders to involve and the most effective way to structure the upcoming meeting.

Vishwa acknowledged the collective wisdom in the room. "Ramji, your unexpected presence has turned this crisis into an opportunity for growth. Your analogy has not only inspired a shift in strategy but has instilled a sense of purpose in our approach. We're grateful for your insights."

Ramji, humbly acknowledging the team's gratitude, shared a final piece of advice. "Remember, just as a garden requires consistent care, so do relationships. Approach this meeting not just as a solution to a problem but as an investment in a partnership. The seeds of understanding and patience you plant today will bear fruits of resilience and growth tomorrow."

As the team prepared to navigate the upcoming meeting and tend to their supplier relationship, the atmosphere in the room transformed. The once tense environment now buzzed with anticipation and determination. The Resilient Alliance, forged through the crucible of challenges, was ready to face the storm together, guided by the wisdom of collaboration and the nurturing spirit of a shared journey.

With Ramji's impactful analogy still echoing in the room, Ajay felt a surge of determination to uncover a solution. Inhaling deeply, he sought approval to dial Anil Kumar, the CEO of the supply chain company. As the speakerphone connected, a tense hush enveloped the room, each person bracing for the pivotal conversation.

Anil's voice emanated from the line, a blend of surprise and anticipation. "Ajay, your call comes earlier than expected. I presume there's more to discuss."

Ajay's demeanor was composed yet empathetic, echoing Ramji's emphasis on seeking understanding. "Indeed, there is much to unravel, considering the challenges we're collectively navigating. I'm eager to hear your perspective. Please be aware that you are on speaker, and our team is present."

Anil's voice carried weariness, as if he had been bracing himself for this conversation. "Ajay, I won't mince words. Our delay in supplying the VR chipsets stems from an ongoing political situation in a country from which we source a critical raw material. The export delay due to the political turmoil has had a domino effect on our entire supply chain."

Ajay listened carefully, his expression thoughtful. "I appreciate your honesty. Can you elaborate on how this situation led to the delay? And why weren't we informed earlier?"

Anil's response was measured, filled with frustration and helplessness. "The delay in the raw material has disrupted our production timelines. As for the lack of communication, it was an error on our part, born from a combination of unforeseen circumstances and operational challenges."

The weight of the situation was noticeable, and the room collectively empathized with Anil's predicament.

Anil's tone carried a tinge of resignation when he said, "In order to secure the contract with Cognos Solutions, we provided the lowest quote, leaving us with thin margins. This was a strategic decision at the time, but it left us with limited capital to navigate through unexpected situations like the one we're currently facing."

There was a moment of silence on the line as Ajay absorbed the Supplier CEO's words and the complexities of the situation. Then, Ajay's voice broke the silence, this time filled with a sense of unity and empathy. "I understand the challenges you're battling, and I can see the tight dependencies that have led us here. Our team feels the urgency of our project, but we also recognize the importance of partnership and shared growth."

Anil's tone seemed to lighten slightly, a mix of surprise and gratitude in his voice. "Ajay, I appreciate your understanding. It's been a tough balancing act, and I regret that it has impacted our commitment to Cognos Solutions."

As Ajay glanced around the room, he could see the shift in his team's perspective. They were no longer just negotiating with a supplier; they were dealing with a fellow professional facing their own set of challenges.

"I'm reminded of Stephen Covey's Win-Win Principle," Ajay mused. "He says it's always possible to craft win-win deals in every situation. I want to approach this from his principles - what can be a win-win deal for both of us?"

Expressing interest, Ajay said, 'We'll get back shortly, Anil" and disconnected the call.

Ajay turned his gaze to Vishwa, the CEO of Cognos. "Vishwa, I'd like to propose a shift from our usual approach. Considering the circumstances and potential cost increases, I believe we should explore a more involved partnership with our supplier."

Vishwa's brows arched in curiosity, encouraging Ajay to delve deeper.

Ajay continued with a voice filled with determination and strategic foresight. "What if we consider investing in our supplier's company? I'll submit a Business Case outlining the immediate, medium, and long-term benefits. This investment could help them overcome financial challenges and ensure a steady supply of the critical raw material. By becoming tangible partners, we not only address the current issue but also foster a relationship built on shared growth."

A contemplative silence filled the room as Vishwa absorbed Ajay's proposal. The idea of investing in a supplier's company was unconventional, yet it held the potential to transform a transactional partnership into a mutually beneficial alliance.

Vishwa responded with measured optimism. "Ajay, I appreciate your innovative thinking and commitment to finding a solution beyond the surface. While this approach needs careful consideration, I believe it aligns with our values of collaboration and fostering lasting partnerships."

The room held its collective breath, awaiting the final decision. Vishwa's gaze shifted towards the team, his expression one of unwavering determination. "Ajay, collaborate closely with the supplier to delve into the intricacies of this investment. Let's ensure our dedication to the project's success remains resolute. I will carefully review your Business Case and present it to the board for approval if it aligns with our strategic vision and objectives."

A sense of accomplishment and unity filled the room as the team realized their journey through this crisis had taken an unexpected turn – one that not only solved an immediate challenge but also laid the foundation for a partnership built on shared growth and resilience.

Soon, Ajay and Vishwa engaged with Anil, expressing their interest in investing in his company. Anil, appreciative of Vishwa's interest, shared the daunting challenges they'd been facing. The sincerity and raw emotion in Anil's voice conveyed years of struggle, sacrifice, and the weight of responsibility he carried.

Anil's voice cracked as he continued, "This means more than you can imagine. It's not just about the company – it's about the families and employees who depend on us. Your willingness to understand our situation and work towards a solution is beyond our expectations."

Vishwa and Ajay sensed Anil's gratitude, feeling the depth of responsibility in the air. The investment they were making went beyond business - it was about lives and livelihoods.

Ajay met Vishwa's eyes, reflecting determination, compassion, and a shared sense of purpose. It wasn't just about profit margins; it was about making a meaningful difference and providing support when it mattered most.

Anil's voice, steadier now but still filled with emotion, continued, "You're not only saving our company but jobs and families from uncertainty and despair. This partnership means more than words can express."

Ajay's response carried a sense of solidarity, "We're in this together. Your challenges are ours, and your success is ours. This alliance transcends contracts; it's about standing by each other, especially when faced with challenges."

Vishwa echoed the sentiment, having listened intently, "We believe in partnerships that uplift and support, especially in times of crisis. Your success is integral to ours, and together, we'll navigate these challenges. I'll need the board's approval to move forward."

The following week unfolded with Ajay and Anil immersed in crafting an investment deal that promised mutual benefits. The proposal, a tapestry of strategic advantages, growth potential, and lasting impact, stood before the board for consideration. After meticulous deliberation, the board bestowed its approval, recognizing the enduring value of fostering such a partnership. It marked a significant moment—a testament to the potency of collaboration, resilience, and the readiness to invest in shared success.

As the meeting to sign the deal commenced, all eyes turned to Ramji, gratitude radiating from the team. "Ramji," Vishwa expressed, echoing the collective sentiments of the team, "your wisdom has been our guiding light through uncharted territory, and your presence has served as a catalyst for transformation. Thank you for illuminating the power of partnership and the remarkable growth that stems from understanding, collaboration, and nurturing."

Ramji responded with humility, his gratitude deeply felt. "It's been an honor to share these principles with all of you. Your openness to embrace them and your dedication to finding solutions that benefit everyone are what truly infuse resilience and endurance into this alliance."

The alliance between Cognos and its supplier unfurled into a captivating mosaic of unforeseen prosperity, weaving together a tale of unexpected success. Routine meetings transcended mere business transactions, morphing into vibrant forums for the exchange of ideas, insights, and personal narratives. The collaborative spark ignited during their crisis meeting continued to weave through their interactions, creating an atmosphere where challenges were confronted collectively, and triumphs were exuberantly celebrated as a unified team.

Takeaways

> **Understanding and Collaboration:** *Emphasis on understanding challenges faced by suppliers before decision-making.*

> *Proposal for open and transparent communication, shifting from transactional to collaborative approaches.*

> **Long-Term Partnership vs. Short-Term Gains:** *Benefits of a collaborative, long-term approach over a competitive, short-term strategy.*

> *Recognition of the value of nurturing relationships, drawing parallels between supplier partnerships and tending a garden.*

- ➢ **Creative Problem-Solving:** *Turning a crisis into an opportunity for growth through creative thinking.*

  Innovative approach of investing in the supplier's company to address financial challenges.

- ➢ **Strategic Decision-Making:** *Ajay showcased strategic brilliance by proposing an empathetic innovation - investing in the supplier's company to address challenges collaboratively.*

  His mastery in securing board approval for this transformative move demonstrated exceptional strategic foresight and persuasive acumen

Attainments

- ➢ **Shifted Perspective:** *Transformation of the team's perspective inspired by the analogy.*

  Shift from seeking new suppliers to understanding and collaborating with the existing one.

- ➢ **Inspired Innovation:** *Proposal of investing in the supplier's company inspired by the emphasis on collaboration and shared growth.*

- ➢ **Catalyst for Transformation:** *Ramji's presence served as a catalyst for transforming the crisis into an opportunity.*

  Fostering a sense of purpose and determination in the team.

Applying the Dynamic 7G Transcendental Framework

Growth:

Emphasis on long-term partnerships and collaborative growth aligned with the Growth aspect of the framework.

Guidance:

Encouragement to understand the supplier's challenges and proposing a collaborative approach.

Grit:

Firm decision to not terminate the agreement and propose an unconventional solution showcased grit and determination.

Gallantry:

Bold move to collaborate even in case of challenges in the partnership demonstrated gallantry and a strategic approach to procurement.

Gratitude:

Team expressed gratitude towards insights, highlighting the importance of gratitude in fostering positive relationships.

Glow:

Renewed sense of purpose and determination in the team, inspired by the analogy, contributing to the Glow aspect of the framework.

Greatness:

Decision to invest in the supplier's company reflected a pursuit of greatness through meaningful partnerships.

"As transcendental professionals, the symphony of change beckons us, inviting a dance through the rhythm of agility. In the grand orchestration of evolution, adaptability becomes the crescendo, crafting a harmonious future where innovation is the melody and resilience, the anthem. Together, an extraordinary transformation awaits at the intersection of agility and evolution, a journey embraced with emotional depth and fervor."

Episode #6:

Beneath the Banyan's Embrace:
A Resonant Symphony of Radical Transformation

In the heart of the Cognos Technologies campus, Ramji stood before a group of eager employees, ready to delve into the intricacies of Agile methodology. The session was held outdoors, under the soothing shade of a banyan tree, where the gentle rustling of leaves added to the tranquility of the moment.

"Agile, my friends," Ramji began with a warm smile, "is not just a methodology, but a mindset; it's a profound philosophy rooted in timeless principles that resonate with the wisdom of great teachers throughout history."

He gestured towards the sprawling banyan tree, its branches extending far and wide. "Consider this tree," he said. "It represents the organic nature of Agile. Just as the tree grows and adapts to its environment, Agile embraces change and evolution."

As Ramji spoke, he painted a vivid picture of Agile's principles using relatable natural metaphors. "Nature teaches us that rigid structures are vulnerable to storms, while flexible ones sway and endure. In Agile, we value individuals and interactions over processes and tools, just as nature values adaptation over rigidity."

He paced beneath the tree's expansive canopy, his voice carrying the wisdom of ages. "Let's talk about transparency," he continued. "In nature, sunlight provides clarity, nourishing life and fostering growth. Similarly, Agile encourages transparency, ensuring that everyone has a clear view of the project's progress and everyone sees the same picture."

Ramji paused to share a real-life example. "Imagine you're on a hike," he said. "You don't plan the entire journey in advance; you adapt to changing terrains and conditions. Agile, too, embraces this adaptive planning. We don't need to have every detail fixed from the outset."

The group nodded in understanding, recognizing the parallels between nature's adaptability and Agile's flexibility.

Ramji's storytelling painted Agile principles with vivid strokes.

"In nature, collaboration among species leads to the ecosystem's harmony," he continued. Ramji's words resonated with the team, and a sense of realization dawned on their faces. The analogy of plants intertwining their roots struck a chord, as they imagined the unseen network beneath the surface, fostering growth and exchange. The notion that proximity and interconnectedness could lead to quicker and healthier development in both plants and humans sparked intrigue.

As Ramji delved into the concept of evolution, drawing parallels between the botanical world and human connections, the team found themselves captivated by the interconnectedness of life. The idea that even the healthy longest-lived humans benefited from close relationships echoed the symbiotic relationships observed in nature. The team recollected the wisdom of interconnectedness Ramji has showered earlier.

Ramji passionately expressed, "Imagine this incredible journey of adaptation and flourishing, much like the way plants connect and prosper through their intricate roots. In a similar vein, living beings, including humans, embark on an ever-evolving odyssey. Our DNA, the very essence of our being, encapsulates the intricate design of our existence, and it's a vibrant code that undergoes continuous transformations.

Cast your thoughts back to humans of 10,000 years past – distinctly different in both physicality and behavior from the vibrant tapestry of humanity today. Evolution unfolds as a mesmerizing dance, an eternal interplay between organisms and the environment, sculpting life to overcome the myriad challenges it encounters."

He emphasized the adaptability of nature and its ability to evolve based on environmental needs. "In essence, the interconnectedness we see in the plant world and the social bonds among humans are both reflections of evolution. Life, in all its forms, adapts to survive and thrive in changing circumstances. It's a beautiful dance of nature, from the microscopic changes in DNA to the macroscopic relationships we form."

The team absorbed these insights, realizing that the principles of interconnectedness and adaptation weren't confined to specific domains but were universal threads woven into the fabric of life itself. As they contemplated the implications of these ideas, a newfound appreciation for the intricate web of life emerged among the team members.

"Similarly, Agile values customer collaboration. We invite feedback and adapt our solutions to meet their evolving needs than focusing more on customer contract negotiations"

As he spoke, Ramji shared a software development case study from Cognos Technologies. "Consider a software project," he began. "In the traditional waterfall approach, everything is meticulously planned upfront. But what if market conditions change? What if the end-users' needs evolve?"

He then contrasted it with an Agile project. "In Agile, we start with a vision, a high-level plan. We build a Minimum Viable Product (MVP), much like a seedling that takes root. We gather feedback early, adapt, and iterate, allowing the project to grow organically, much like a tree branches out in response to the environment."

Agile, my friends, is not just a method; it's a reflection of the wisdom of nature. It teaches us to adapt, collaborate, and embrace change—just as life has done for millennia. Let Agile be our compass as we navigate the ever-changing landscape of technology and business."

Ramji, sensing the curiosity of his audience, decided to delve a little deeper into the history of Agile. He had always believed that understanding the roots of a methodology enriched the learning experience.

"Now, as we journey into the world of Agile," he began, "let's also explore how this methodology came into being. Agile, my friends, is a product of collaboration and innovation, much like the principles it stands for."

He paused for a moment, letting his words sink in. "In the early 2000s," he continued, "the software development landscape was plagued by inefficiencies and frustrations. Large-scale projects often ran over budget and beyond their planned timelines. The traditional 'waterfall' approach, which involved rigid planning and sequential phases, simply wasn't cutting it anymore."

Ramji could see the team nodding in agreement. They had likely encountered similar challenges in their own work.

"So," Ramji went on, "a group of visionary software developers, representing different methodologies and philosophies, came together to find a better way. They met at a ski resort in Utah and, over a few days, crafted the Agile Manifesto."

He emphasized the word 'Manifesto' as if underscoring its significance. "This manifesto," he explained, "outlined a set of guiding values and principles for software development. It prioritized individuals and interactions over processes, working solutions over documentations, customer collaboration over contract negotiations and adapting to change over following a plan."

The team listened intently, recognizing the shift in mindset that Agile represented.

"The Agile Manifesto," Ramji continued, "also introduced us to twelve principles that underpin Agile methodologies, principles like satisfying customers through early and continuous delivery of valuable software and welcoming changing requirements, even late in development."

The air in the room crackled with the excitement of newfound knowledge, and Vishwa eagerly thrust his hand into the air. "Ramji," he inquired, "what prompted this shift to Agile? What challenges was it designed to tackle?"

Ramji acknowledged with a nod, truly valuing Vishwa's thought-provoking query. "The pivot to Agile became imperative as the conventional methods of software development found themselves grappling to match the ever-evolving dynamics of the industry. Projects frequently faced delays, and by the time they reached fruition, the market landscape had already shifted. Agile stepped in to tackle these challenges head-on, putting a premium on adaptability, collaboration, and the iterative delivery of value to customers."

The team continued to engage with Ramji, their questions and discussions painting a more vivid picture of Agile's history and principles. It was clear that they were not just learning about a mindset; they were embracing a philosophy that could revolutionize their approach to work.

Recognizing the essence of embracing Agile principles through hands-on practice, he embarked on a transformative initiative known as "Agile Week.", typically a 'Scrum' week as Ramji derived Scrum framework was more suitable for the team. This innovative concept sought to immerse the team in practical experiences, going beyond traditional learning methods. The core idea was to create a dynamic balance between Ramji's insightful sessions and real-world application throughout the week.

Ramji animatedly shared, "Agile Week won't be your typical sit-down-all-day affair. It's about infusing learning with action. Picture a dynamic blend of interactive sessions, hands-on workshops, and engaging activities. The aim? To let everyone dive into Agile principles in a hands-on manner, tackling real tasks that showcase the power of Agile methodologies."

To quell any worries about daily responsibilities, Ramji laid out a schedule featuring 3-hour sessions each day. He reassured the team, noting, "I get it – we need to strike a balance between immersing ourselves in Agile and handling our day-to-day tasks. That's why we've planned focused sessions from 6 to 9 am every day of the Agile week. This dedicated time slot lets you experience Agile without sacrificing your regular work commitments. It's structured to be effective and respectful of your ongoing tasks."

This innovative approach ensured that team members could actively participate in Agile activities during specific hours, leaving the remainder of the day free for their usual work. Ramji highlighted the tangible application of Agile principles, envisioning a seamless integration into their daily workflow.

"Let's talk about the significance of a week," Ramji began, a playful glint in his eye. "It's not too short to grasp Agile's essence, nor is it too long to be overwhelming. It's the Goldilocks of time frames – just right for immersing ourselves in Agile practices."

Pausing for emphasis, Ramji declared, "And guess what? I'm taking the reins for the upcoming Agile Week." His mischievous twinkle hinted at a week filled with excitement and transformative experiences.

The team leaned in, their curiosity piqued, as the Agile Coach left the statement hanging in the air, a promise of more Agile adventures to come from 6 am the next Monday.

Day 1

Setting the Agile Stage - Backlog as the Script

The Cognos Technologies campus hummed with anticipation as Ramji, their esteemed leader, geared up to step into the role of Agile coach for the week.

"Let's kick off our Agile Week with the recognition that every successful Agile project needs a well-defined stage to set the scene," declared Ramji. "Just like in a captivating theatrical performance, we require clarity and alignment before the action unfolds."

The Cognos platform team, a dynamic blend of department and business leaders, developers, product owners, business analysts, DevOps engineers, testers, AI team members, compliance experts, and marketing professionals, leaned in, enthralled by Ramji's words. While they had been diligently shaping their innovative gaming platform, Agile Week promised a fresh perspective and an opportunity to truly embrace Agile principles.

Guided by Ramji's expert hand, the team dedicated the day to crystallizing the vision for their product.

Vishal, the lead developer, infused his words with passion as he articulated their vision for creating an immersive, user-centric gaming experience. Priya, the diligent product owner, underscored the importance of delivering features that genuinely resonated with their gaming community. The team collectively defined OKRs. (Objectives and Key Results), ensuring that every item in the product backlog was strategically aligned with these OKRs. and the overarching vision of Cognos to become the most respected virtual gaming company globally.

"Together," Ramji emphasized, "we'll craft a product backlog—a meticulously prioritized list of features and requirements. Think of it as the script for our Agile play. This backlog will be our guiding force, ensuring that our actions stay laser-focused on the project's objectives."

He passionately highlighted the significance of securing the business team's approval for the prioritized product backlog by the Product Owner, after necessary negotiations before the day's close—an integral facet of our Agile methodology. This ensures seamless alignment and keeps our Agile practices at their prime.

The team marveled at how this approach seamlessly aligned everyone's focus on the project's goals and objectives. It marked a significant departure from their past experiences, where rigid plans often stifled creativity. Agile was proving to be a breath of fresh air, allowing them the flexibility to adapt and innovate as needed.

As the session drew to a close, the team departed with a profound sense of purpose. Agile Week had kicked off with the stage impeccably set, and they eagerly anticipated the unfolding drama of the second day of the Agile week.

Day 2

Sprint Planning - Bringing the Agile Play to Life

As the sun painted the second day of Agile Week with hues of promise, the Cognos Technologies Agile team gathered, brimming with anticipation. Under Ramji's guiding light, a fresh purpose had taken root within them.

Today's agenda delved into the heart of Agile methodology—sprint planning.

"Welcome to day two," Ramji declared, his eyes reflecting the enthusiasm mirrored in the team. "Think of a sprint as a distinct act in our Agile play—a set time-frame where a nimble, cross-functional team choreographs a series of user stories."

The team converged eagerly for the sprint planning session. Rahul, the meticulous tester, wore his excitement unabashedly. The prospect of condensed development cycles and frequent chances to deliver value resonated like sweet music in his ears.

Product owner, Priya, curated a collection of user stories from the product backlog, carefully chosen for their priority and potential impact. These were the scenes they aimed to spotlight in this act of their Agile journey.

Adhering to the INVEST principle (Independent, Negotiable, Valuable, Estimable, Small and Testable), they meticulously prepared and structured their stories, laying the foundation for efficient execution. This approach aligned seamlessly with Agile's core tenets of adaptability and iterative progress.

Ramji, the maestro of this Agile symphony, advised the team on assigning story points based on significance and complexity. He underscored that the complexity-to-story-point ratio might vary, reflecting the developer's expertise. These story points served as the currency for allotting tasks, with the team operating at an 80% capacity, leaving a 20% buffer for unforeseen challenges. He even explained how any why the Fibonacci series was used in story pointing.

With crystal-clear objectives—to deliver a potentially shippable increment of the virtual gaming platform by sprint's end—Ramji stressed the pivotal role of confirming the approval of backlog prioritization by the business team. "Our delivery is to the business, our internal customer," he clarified, "and they, in turn, release it to external customers on demand. Their approval for our prioritization is paramount, apart from 'alignment'"

"Our stage is set," Ramji continued, a smile playing on his lips, "and now, we're rehearsing the scenes. Each story unfolds as a unique act in our Agile play. By sprint's end, we aim to present a compelling act that speaks volumes."

With the sprint plan meticulously laid out, the team eagerly embraced the next phase of Agile Week. Soon, daily standup meetings would become a routine, and the unwritten story of the sprint's progress awaited its vibrant narration.

Day 3-6

Daily Standups and Sprint Execution - A New Agile Play Each Day

The Agile Week entered its third day, and the stage was set for dynamic action. The team, having rehearsed their roles, now delved into the heart of Agile—engaging in daily standup meetings and sprint execution.

Beneath the embracing branches of the banyan tree, Ramji conveyed the significance of these rituals to the team. "From days three to six of this Agile Week, we sync with the Agile rhythm, conducting daily standups and honing in on sprint execution. A key to our success is concurrent testing, allowing developers to tackle defects alongside their daily tasks, boosting our chances of reaching the sprint goal."

"These standups are like the heartbeat of our project, keeping us in sync and ready to face challenges. During the sprint, we allocate time to plan for the next one, assigning story points for better estimation. It's crucial to foresee technical challenges and adopt a proactive approach to avoid unexpected issues during the sprint. Creating an environment where every team member feels comfortable expressing concerns fosters open communication and collaborative problem-solving, embodying the Agile spirit of teamwork."

Each day, beneath the same banyan tree, the team convened for a brief standup. These meetings mirrored actors gathering backstage before a performance—a chance to discuss progress, challenges, and plans for the day.

As updates flowed, it became clear how these daily check-ins nurtured collaboration and transparency. All were aligned toward the sprint goal, swiftly addressing any hurdles. This marked a departure from past experiences where communication languished in silos.

Sneha, a problem-solving developer, shared her progress with enthusiasm. "I've made strides in the user authentication feature, enhancing the security of our gaming platform."

Rahul, the meticulous tester, valued the transparency of the Agile process. "Identifying and reporting bugs early will lead to a more stable product and minimize the technical debts in the long run."

Agile Week unfolded, and the team's synergy became palpable. They collaborated seamlessly, driven by the sprint goal and Ramji's guiding hand. The excitement of delivering value to their gaming community fueled their motivation.

In this phase, the true power of Agile began to shine. The team experienced the benefits of shorter development cycles, rapid feedback loops, and a shared sense of purpose. Each day was a new scene in their Agile play, and they delivered their best performance with enthusiasm and precision.

Demo Day Finale: Showcasing Agile Brilliance

The much-anticipated final day of Agile Week had arrived. It was time for the team to showcase what they had accomplished during the sprint and reflect on how they could inspect, improve, and adapt. Ramji gathered the team under the familiar banyan tree, and the atmosphere was charged with excitement. "On the final day," Ramji explained, "we hold a demo. It's a chance to showcase what we've accomplished during the sprint and to inspect and adapt on how we can improve."

The team was eager to share their achievements. Vishal, the lead developer, stepped up to the virtual stage and began demonstrating the new gameplay mechanics they had implemented. The Product Owner, Priya, watched intently, offering feedback and praise.

"Excellent work," Priya exclaimed. "Our gaming community will love these new features! and the beta testers provided valuable insights that helped us shape these improvements."

With each feature showcased in front of the group of department and business leaders, developers, product owners, business analysts, DevOps engineers, testers, AI team members, compliance experts, and marketing professionals team, the room buzzed with energy. The team had indeed delivered a compelling act in their Agile play, just as Ramji had envisioned.

In this scenario, Vishwa, the enthusiastic Business Leader, in this case, eagerly witnessed the progress he had imagined. Holding back his comments until the culmination of the agile sessions, he simply exclaimed, "Good job," leaving a sense of anticipation lingering in the air.

Retrospective Reflections - Learning from the Play

After the exhilarating sprint review, the atmosphere buzzed with anticipation as the team huddled in a circle for the retrospective.

Guiding the discussion, Ramji set the stage for reflection, saying, "In the retrospective, we delve into the triumphs of the sprint and pinpoint areas for enhancement in the upcoming one."

In the vibrant exchange of ideas, Sneha championed the notion of investing extra time in honing our user stories—a sentiment that found a harmonious chord with many minds. Rahul brought the spotlight onto the pivotal role of automated testing in the quest for a more streamlined development process. The team's remarkable openness to feedback and their steadfast dedication to perpetual enhancement radiated through every discussion.

Under Ramji's guidance, not only were the feedback and action items meticulously documented, but they were also swiftly delegated to the responsible task owners. Ramji also instructed that the progress on each item was vigilantly tracked and expedited to closure, embodying the team's commitment to constant evolution.

Ramji then introduced the concept of NoOps. With enthusiasm, he expressed, "Introducing NoOps is like cultivating a self-sustaining ecosystem in nature. In a vibrant forest, each element seamlessly functions without constant intervention. Trees grow, animals navigate, and the ecosystem adapts, all without a central orchestrator.

In the same vein, NoOps aspires to create a self-regulating software environment where automated processes synchronize, diminishing the need for perpetual manual involvement. It mirrors the equilibrium found in nature, where the system thrives efficiently, yielding optimal results with minimal interference."

During Agile Week, department and business leaders like Vishwa, Rohan, and Aditi embraced a hands-off approach, allowing their teams to collaborate freely without intervention. This fostered an environment where teams had the freedom to share thoughts and ideas openly, enhancing the spirit of Agile collaboration.

As the sun gracefully dipped below the horizon on Agile Week, the Agile team reconvened beneath the sheltering banyan tree. They had not merely witnessed but actively participated in experiencing the Agile principles, led by Ramji with an Agile Coach's hat. The true significance of the week had unfolded—it wasn't just a timeframe; it was a voyage marked by collaboration, adaptation, and unwavering dedication to continuous improvement.

Agile's Ongoing Symphony: From Week to Work Life

"The week might be drawing to a close," Ramji declared, "but our Agile expedition is just setting sail. Let's carry these principles and practices forward as we navigate the ever-shifting landscape of technology and business."

Ramji continued...

"In our exploration of Agile principles, it's vital to grasp that our ultimate destination is the creation of self-managing teams. We don't aspire to a scenario where someone dictates every move. Instead, we aim for a team capable of collaboration, effective task planning, execution, reflective practices, continuous improvement—an Agile dance.

In Agile, we entrust the expertise and creativity of our team members. Our insights, ideas, and decision-making prowess are valued drivers for project progression. Armed with the principles we've absorbed, we possess the tools to take ownership of our work, collectively steering our projects in the right direction.

As we press on in this Agile journey, remember we're not merely adhering to a set of rules; we are evolving into self-managing professionals adept at adapting to challenges, collaborating effectively, and delivering exceptional value. This is how we'll flourish in the ever-evolving landscape of technology and business.

Having harnessed Agile's transformative power, our path forward becomes clear. Our goal is to cultivate a work environment where self-management is the norm, echoing the intricate harmony found in nature.

Like a decentralized ecosystem where each organism plays a crucial role, we envision every team member actively contributing to our projects' success. It involves collaborative efforts, efficient task execution, constant reflection, and a commitment to continuous improvement—a cycle akin to the self-regulating systems seen in the natural world.

We place unwavering trust in our expertise and creativity, empowering us to make informed decisions that steer our projects towards triumph."

Armed with a newfound understanding and a taste of Agile practices, the team departed Agile Week with a sense of purpose, ready to apply these principles to their real-world projects and product development. Agile was no longer a concept; it was a way of working and thinking that would transform their approach to projects, product development and innovation.

After Agile Week's conclusion, the Cognos Technologies agile team seamlessly integrated the learned Agile principles into their work life. Ramji's guidance left a lasting impact, and the team is resolute in applying their newfound knowledge.

Daily Standups

The team seamlessly incorporated daily standup meetings into their regular routine. These brief check-ins allowed them to maintain transparency and alignment, just as they had during Agile Week. It became a valuable practice for addressing challenges promptly and ensuring everyone stayed focused on their daily tasks as well as product and project goals.

Iterative Development

The concept of breaking product development into smaller, manageable chunks resonated with the team. They began to adopt iterative development, working on smaller increments of their projects & product development and gathering feedback along the way. This approach not only improved efficiency but also ensured that the end product better met user needs.

Embracing Change

Agile had taught them to embrace change rather than resist it. They no longer feared evolving requirements or market shifts. Instead, they welcomed these changes as opportunities to deliver greater value to their customers.

Continuous Improvement

The retrospective process, practiced during Agile Week, became a regular part of their project and product development cycles. The team met after each sprint to discuss what had gone well and what could be improved. This commitment to continuous improvement led to a culture of learning and growth.

Customer Collaboration

Agile's emphasis on customer collaboration was transformative. The team actively sought feedback from their gaming community and engaged them in the development process. This not only improved the quality of their products but also built a loyal user base.

The Business Owner's Applause - Tangible Results of Agile

As the months unfolded, the MVP emerged, and Agile principles seamlessly became woven into the very fabric of the team's identity. The results were not just evident; they were transformative.

Projects and products flowed with newfound speed, sporting fewer defects, and perfectly synchronized with user expectations. This wasn't merely a shift; it was a revolution.

In the wake of tangible success, the team emerged as a powerhouse, steering the company towards triumph. The realization dawned that customer contentment and team morale weren't just checkboxes but pillars of excellence. The team wasn't just working; they were crafting a legacy of success.

Enter Vishwa, the Business Owner, who could sense the palpable progress and found genuine delight in the team's achievements. He grasped the true value of the Agile approach, witnessing its positive ripples across project outcomes.

Fuelled by Vishwa's appreciation, the team harnessed newfound motivation, propelling them to outshine in subsequent sprints. This wasn't just a win; it was a testament to the profound impact of customer satisfaction. The dual satisfaction, stemming from the team's unwavering commitment to improvement and their prowess in delivering value efficiently, became the cornerstone of their journey.

The expedition into the Agile realm, particularly through the lens of the Scrum framework, transcended a mere week-long event. It morphed into a paradigm shift, reshaping how the Cognos Technologies team approached their craft. They weren't just agile in methodology but in mindset – a force ready to adapt, innovate, and thrive amidst the ever-evolving landscape of technology and business. The journey wasn't just a transformation; it was their evolution into a powerhouse of agility and success.

Kanban Board- A Visual Symphony of Workflow

Ramji became the driving force behind the transformative potential of the Kanban board, shaping it into a vibrant visual compass that guided our expedition. He declared, "This ingenious board seamlessly wove itself into the fabric of our workflow, evolving into the pulsating core that empowered us to identify bottlenecks with a mere glance and deftly maneuver around them. It stands as our vigilant guardian, not only ensuring the hallowed boundaries of Work In Progress (WIP) limits were met but held in reverence, shielding our team from the dangers of both overwhelm and under-utilization."

The Lasting Echo of Agile Week

Ramji highlighted the abundance of frameworks available to cater to various implementation needs within agile methodologies. He emphasized his primary goal of fostering the agile mindset and introduced the Scrum framework, citing its alignment with Cogno's existing delivery strategy.

And so, the legacy of Agile Week lived on, not just as a memory but as a catalyst for lasting change and innovation at Cognos Technologies. The team had truly embraced the Agile way, incorporating Scrum and utilizing Kanban boards, and their future looked brighter than ever.

Takeaways

> **Agile as a Mindset:** *Emphasizing Agile as a mindset rooted in timeless principles, not a methodology.*

> **Organic Nature of Agile:** *The banyan tree metaphor to convey Agile's embrace of change and evolution, similar to nature.*

> **Value of Adaptability:** *Value adaptability over rigidity, drawing parallels with nature's vulnerability of rigid structures.*

> **Transparency in Agile:** *Relate sunlight providing clarity in nature to Agile's encouragement of transparency in project progress.*

➤ **Adaptive Planning:** *Agile doesn't require fixed plans but adapts to changing conditions, drawing from hiking experiences.*

➤ **Collaboration in Nature and Agile:** *Draw parallels between collaboration in nature leading to harmony and Agile's emphasis on customer collaboration.*

➤ **Evolution in Nature and Human Connections:** *Link the adaptability of nature to human evolution, stressing the importance of interconnectedness.*

➤ **Agile's Historical Context:** *Understanding the origin of Agile in response to inefficiencies in traditional waterfall methods in the early 2000s.*

➤ **Agile Manifesto:** *Agile Manifesto and its guiding values and principles for software development.*

➤ **Agile Week Concept:** *Concept of Agile Week, aiming for a dynamic balance between theory and hands-on practice.*

➤ **Setting the Agile Stage:** *Importance of a well-defined stage for Agile projects and the need for clarity and alignment.*

➤ **Sprint Planning:** *Concept of sprint planning, equating it to choreographing scenes in an Agile play.*

➤ **Daily Standups and Sprint Execution:** *Emphasize the heartbeat of the project in daily standups, focusing on collaboration and transparency.*

➤ **Demo Day Finale:** *Significance of showcasing accomplishments on the final day and reflecting on improvements.*

➤ **Retrospective Reflections:** *Retrospective sessions to reflect on the sprint, discuss triumphs, and identify areas for enhancement.*

➤ **Continuous Improvement:** *Encourage a culture of continuous improvement, adopting feedback and iterating on processes.*

➤ **Customer Collaboration:** *Agile's emphasis on customer collaboration, involving end-users in the development process.*

➢ **NoOps Concept:** *Concept of NoOps, aiming for a self-regulating software environment.*

Attainments

➢ **Implementation of Agile Principles:** *Successfully implemented Agile principles through storytelling and real-world examples.*

➢ **Introduction of Agile Week:** *Introduced and successfully executed the concept of Agile Week, combining theory and hands-on practice.*

➢ **Integration of Agile into Work Life:** *Guided the team in seamlessly integrating Agile principles into their regular work life.*

➢ **Transformation of Team Dynamics:** *Catalyzed a paradigm shift in the team's approach to projects, fostering adaptability and innovation.*

➢ **Success in Sprint Execution:** *Led the team to successfully execute sprints, focusing on iterative development and frequent value delivery.*

➢ **Cultivation of Continuous Improvement:** *Established a culture of continuous improvement through regular retrospective sessions.*

➢ **Customer Satisfaction and Collaboration:** *Ensured active customer collaboration, resulting in higher customer satisfaction and a loyal user base.*

➢ **Introduction of Kanban:** *Successfully implemented Kanban boards as a visual compass to guide workflow and identify bottlenecks.*

➢ **Legacy of Agile Week:** *Left a lasting legacy of Agile transformation, instigating lasting change and innovation in the team.*

Applying the Dynamic 7G Transcendental Framework

Growth:

Fostered growth by introducing Agile principles, promoting continuous improvement, and embracing change.

Guidance:

Provided guidance through storytelling, real-world examples, and the Agile Week initiative, guiding the team in Agile practices.

Grit:

Demonstrated grit by addressing challenges in traditional methodologies and steering the team towards Agile transformation.

Gallantry:

Showed gallantry by leading the team through the transformative Agile journey, taking ownership of the process.

Gratitude:

Encouraged a culture of gratitude through open communication, collaboration, and appreciation for feedback.

Glow:

Instilled a sense of enthusiasm and energy through engaging sessions, Agile Week, and the visual aspect of Kanban boards.

Greatness:

Aiming for greatness by cultivating a self-managing team, promoting collaboration, and achieving tangible success.

"Amidst the relentless blaze of corporate challenges, where flames of adversity flicker, transcendental professionals rise. Unyielding in the heat, transformation unfolds. The passionate forge of those flames shapes resolute goals. Through the inferno, not unscathed, but fortified, the journey unfolds towards the radiant fulfillment of shared aspirations."

Episode #7:

Stormy Crossroads: Navigating Regulatory Rapids

The Cognos Technologies boardroom, typically a place for strategic discussions and decision-making, had turned into a battleground of tension and uncertainty. The top executives, including the CEO, Product & Technical Heads, and Legal advisors, were gathered around a polished oak table, their expressions etched with concern as the CEO began to read the letter that had just arrived, bearing the formidable seal of the regulatory body.

"Ladies and gentlemen, we have a situation," the CEO announced, his voice betraying a hint of unease. All eyes in the room were fixed on the letter.

The contents of the letter were nothing short of a regulatory nightmare. It spelled out a series of exhaustive assessments, stringent tests, and compliance checks that the company's soon-to-be-launched product would have to undergo. The timeline for these procedures remained conspicuously absent, casting a dark cloud of uncertainty over the product's imminent launch.

The Legal Head, Mr. Bhushan, a man known for his unshakable composure, leaned forward, his steely gaze narrowing as he scrutinized the document. "This is highly irregular. I've seen my fair share of regulatory challenges, but never something of this magnitude and on such short notice."

A sense of disbelief swept through the room. "This is catastrophic," one executive declared, their voice trembling with frustration. "We've poured everything we have into this product, and now it's hanging by a thread."

Rohan, a pragmatic voice within the organization, leaned forward, his expression a mix of determination and concern. "We're at crossroads; we can either comply with these demands, which could mean an indefinite delay, or we can stand up and fight for our vision."

Mr. Bhushan, the legal expert, interjected with a note of caution, "Compliance is the path of least resistance, but it's also shrouded in ambiguity. We must explore every legal avenue available to us, even if it means going up against a formidable regulatory body. It won't be easy, but it might be our only way forward."

The legal advisors exchanged glances, fully aware of the complexity and stakes involved. One of them spoke, his tone unwavering. "This is not just a regulatory hiccup. It's a battle for our identity and the principles we stand for."

The room seemed to pulsate with tension as the weight of the decision hung heavy in the air. It was a defining moment in Cognos Technologies' history, a moment that would test their resolve and their unwavering commitment to their groundbreaking product.

As the discussion continued, arguments flared, voices were raised, and heated debates ensued. Some executives argued vehemently for compliance, fearing the repercussions of challenging the regulatory body. Others, fueled by the passion for their innovation, were resolute in their determination to fight for their vision.

Vishwa's frustration was palpable as he leaned forward and asked the question that weighed heavily on everyone's mind. "What have we done wrong? How did we end up in this regulatory quagmire?"

Mr. Bhushan, adjusted his glasses and sighed. "Vishwa, it's not a matter of right or wrong on our part. The issue lies in the outdated regulations governing the tech sector. These laws were crafted in an era that predates the rapid advancements we've witnessed in technology. Consequently, they've left a vast gray area that is now ensnaring us."

He took a moment, crafting his words thoughtfully. "Ever thought about moving our company from Hyderabad to Gibraltar? Gibraltar boasts a robust regulatory system for online gaming. The Gibraltar Regulatory Authority (GRA) ensures licensing and regulation, offering a solid and esteemed haven for gaming companies."

The room fell into a contemplative silence, the weight of the decision hanging heavily. Relocating to Gibraltar would involve substantial logistical and operational challenges, but it was becoming increasingly clear that their current path was fraught with uncertainty and potential setbacks.

Vishwa, known for his ability to think on his feet, spoke again, his tone laced with concern. "If we do decide to relocate, what happens to our vision, our commitment to innovation? Are we just running away from a battle we should fight?"

The legal advisors exchanged glances, understanding the gravity of Vishwa's question. It wasn't just a matter of convenience or regulatory ease; it was about the core principles and values that Cognos Technologies held dear.

Aditi pushed back, her eyes reflecting determination. "Our vision shouldn't crumble beneath the bureaucratic burden. Yet, we can't disregard the dangers of defying regulators. It's a delicate balancing act, a dance on the edge of a double-edged sword."

Vishwa, expressing his mounting frustration, exclaimed, "This is beyond reason! The regulatory head is being utterly unreasonable. We might need to seriously weigh our options, including relocation to Gibraltar. When you think about our business survival, the impact on stakeholders, our ability to adapt to change, and the certainty of legal and operational aspects, it seems like Gibraltar could offer a more favorable environment for our company."

Just as the discussion seemed to be spiraling into an unresolvable conflict, someone in the room suggested, "We need a fresh perspective. Let's invite Ramji. His wisdom has guided us through challenges before."

Nods of agreement followed, and a message was swiftly sent to Ramji, who had been apprised of the situation. He arrived at the boardroom in 90 minutes, his presence commanding attention and respect. The room fell into a heavy silence as he took his seat at the table.

Vishwa, his expression a mix of hope and anxiety, began, "Ramji, we find ourselves in a dire situation. Our product launch, the culmination of years of innovation, is at stake due to unforeseen regulatory hurdles. We're torn between complying, which might mean an indefinite delay, or relocating to Gibraltar, which poses its own challenges."

Vishwa continued, "I remember a company ZebPay, once one of the leading cryptocurrency exchanges in India, faced difficulties due to regulatory uncertainties and challenges in the cryptocurrency space. In 2018, the Reserve Bank of India (RBI), the country's central bank, imposed a banking ban that prohibited banks from providing services to cryptocurrency exchanges and traders. Zebpay moved to Singapore and now is one of the significant players in the crypto industry."

Ramji nodded, his serene demeanor a stark contrast to the turmoil in the room. "I understand the gravity of the situation we all are facing. It reminds me of a story, one that Buddha shared when faced with a skeptic."

Ramji began, "Once, Buddha was traveling to a neighboring village where he would deliver his sermon daily and return by evening. On his way, he encountered a skeptic eager to test his wisdom. The skeptic presented Buddha with a potted plant and posed a challenging question, 'Will this plant survive tomorrow?'"

"Buddha, possessing innate insight, immediately grasped the skeptic's intentions. If he predicted the plant's survival, the skeptic would likely pluck it to prove him wrong. Conversely, if he foresaw its demise, the skeptic might tend to it, again challenging Buddha's prediction. Undeterred, Buddha calmly gazed at the plant and replied, 'It will live.'"

The room was captivated by the unfolding story, with curiosity evident in every face.

Ramji continued, "True to his intent to test Buddha, the skeptic plucked the plant with a triumphant smile. Unfazed by this act, Buddha continued his journey with equanimity."

"That night," Ramji's voice carried the weight of the story's profound message, "a fierce storm swept over the village, burying the plant beneath a layer of mud. Against all odds, the plant not only survived but thrived. When Buddha returned the next day along the same path, the skeptic, humbled by the plant's resilience, fell at his feet in sincere apology."

"Buddha," Ramji continued, his gaze steady and penetrating, "with his wisdom, reminded the skeptic that he was not a deity capable of altering the plant's fate. He had merely observed the plant's energy—and he saw a strong will to live."

"If it wants to live," Buddha said as his voice deepened, "neither I nor you can truly destroy it."

"Even the storm," Buddha's tone softened, as if unveiling a profound revelation, "was used by the plant to survive."

Ramji's words hung in the air, and the room fell into a contemplative silence. The parable served as a poignant reminder that challenges, even the most formidable ones, could be harnessed as opportunities for growth and resilience.

Vishwa, his frustration still fresh, found himself reevaluating his earlier stance. Perhaps, just as the plant had used the storm to survive, they could find a way to thrive in the face of this regulatory tempest.

With Ramji's guidance and the newfound determination of the leadership team, a plan of action was swiftly put into motion. Ramji decided to employ a Socratic approach, inviting different perspectives through thoughtful questioning.

Ramji: "Let's consider the core values that define Cognos Technologies. What do we stand for as a company?"

Aditi: "Innovation, pushing boundaries, and creating groundbreaking products."

Ramji: "Exactly. Now, in the face of regulatory challenges, how do we align our values with the decisions we make? Do we compromise on innovation, or do we find a way to uphold our principles?"

Rohan: "We can't compromise on innovation. It's what sets us apart."

Ramji: "Agreed. Now, let's explore the options before us. Compliance seems like the path of least resistance, but does it truly align with our commitment to innovation?"

Bhushan: "Compliance might stifle our innovation, but challenging the regulators is risky."

Ramji: "Risk is inherent in innovation. Now, considering the regulatory landscape, can we influence change from within or are we compelled to consider relocation?"

Vishwa: "Relocating might be a drastic step, but if it ensures our vision survives, should we dismiss it outright?"

Ramji's questioning continued, navigating through the complexities of their situation. Each question prompted the team to delve deeper into their values, aspirations, and the pragmatic realities they faced.

In a series of intense brainstorming sessions, the team engaged in a Socratic dialogue. Their discussions were filled with passion and conviction, with Ramji facilitating a process that encouraged critical thinking.

As the Socratic discussions unfolded, Ramji and the team decided to form a committee of experts from various industries. This diverse group of individuals was tasked with creating a memorandum that would apprise the lawmakers of the gravity of the situation.

Ms. Kapoor, one of the prominent venture capitalists in the committee, emphasized, "Let's craft a narrative that not only highlights Cognos but addresses the broader issues in the tech industry. It's not just about us; it's about the entire nation's potential."

The CEO of a successful tech startup, Mr. Deshmukh, added, "We need to appeal to their sense of national pride. This is about India's position on the global stage."

Under Ramji's guidance, the committee engaged in a series of Socratic discussions to refine their arguments. Questions like "How does Cognos contribute to the nation's tech prowess?" and "What's the larger impact of stifling innovation through outdated regulations?" guided their narrative.

When the day came to present their case to the head of state, known for being industry-friendly and forward-thinking, Ramji led the charge. The Socratic approach had laid the groundwork for a compelling narrative.

Ramji: "Your Excellency, our product represents not just the innovation of Cognos but the very spirit of India's tech prowess. If we can navigate these regulatory rapids, we can propel our nation to the forefront of the global tech revolution."

The head of state, recognizing the gravity of the situation, leaned forward. "This is a turning point. Let's ensure we don't miss this opportunity."

The Socratic questioning had influenced the lawmakers' perspective. They swiftly initiated discussions to amend the outdated regulations that had caused the regulatory roadblock. The power of collaboration and advocacy, guided by the Socratic approach, became evident.

In the legislative chambers, as the discussions on legal amendments grew more intense, emotions ran high:

One lawmaker, echoing the sentiments of many, declared, "We can't afford to hold back our tech industry with outdated laws. It's time for change."

Another added, "Cognos Technologies has shown us what's possible. Let's not be the ones to hinder progress."

The regulatory body's case against Cognos Technologies was withdrawn. It was a pivotal moment—a sign that change was on the horizon. The outdated regulations were replaced with more progressive and industry-friendly laws, aligning with the needs of modern technology companies.

Ramji, the committee members, and the entire leadership team at Cognos Technologies celebrated not only their victory but also the triumph of innovation over adversity. They had not only navigated the regulatory rapids but had also paved the way for a more conducive environment for tech innovation in India.

In the end, Vishwa approached Ramji with emotions welling up in his eyes. "Ramji, I can't find the words to express my gratitude for your unwavering leadership through this tumultuous journey."

Ramji, his face reflecting the depth of the moment, invoked the story of Buddha and the plant's will to live one last time. "Vishwa, just as that plant harnessed the storm to survive, Cognos demonstrated an indomitable spirit. We observed the energy, the will, and the determination to thrive, even in the face of the storm. That's the essence of what makes our company exceptional."

With the storm conquered and the dawn of a new era for Cognos Technologies, their unyielding spirit remained the beacon that guided them forward, undeterred by any challenges that lay ahead.

Takeaways

➢ **Harnessing Challenges as Opportunities:** *Challenges, even formidable ones, can be opportunities for growth and resilience.*

Illustrated through the story of Buddha and the plant's will to live despite facing a storm.

➢ **Aligning Values with Decisions:** *Encouragement to reflect on Cognos Technologies' core values, emphasizing innovation, pushing boundaries, and creating groundbreaking products.*

Urged leadership to align their values with decisions, questioning whether compliance truly aligned with their commitment to innovation.

➢ **Socratic Approach:** *Implementation of a Socratic approach in decision-making, fostering critical thinking and thoughtful questioning.*

Intense brainstorming sessions engaged the team in a Socratic dialogue to navigate through the complexities of the situation.

- **Collaboration and Advocacy:** *Formation of a committee of experts under Ramji's guidance.*

  Advocacy for a collaborative approach in crafting a narrative that highlighted Cognos Technologies and addressed broader issues in the tech industry.

  Collaboration with lawmakers using a Socratic approach to influence their perspective and initiate discussions for amending outdated regulations.

- **National Pride and Industry Impact:** *Emphasis on the broader impact of stifling innovation through outdated regulations on the nation's tech prowess.*

  Committee urged lawmakers to appeal to their sense of national pride, positioning Cognos Technologies as a representative of India's position on the global stage.

- **Persistence and Determination:** *Demonstration of persistence and determination in the face of adversity.*

  Guided the leadership team to observe the energy, will, and determination within Cognos Technologies, akin to the plant's will to live in the face of a storm.

Attainments

- **Regulatory Victory:** *Successful navigation of regulatory challenges by influencing lawmakers and initiating discussions to amend outdated regulations.*

  Regulatory body's case against Cognos Technologies was withdrawn, signifying a pivotal moment and a triumph of innovation over adversity.

- **Change in Legislative Landscape:** *Key role played in changing the legislative landscape by advocating for more progressive and industry-friendly laws.*

Contribution to replacing outdated regulations with laws that aligned with the needs of modern technology companies.

➤ **Preservation of Core Values:** *Ensured that Cognos Technologies didn't compromise on its core values, especially innovation, even in the face of regulatory hurdles.*

Preserved the company's commitment to pushing boundaries and creating groundbreaking products.

➤ **Establishment of a Collaborative Committee:** *Establishment of a diverse committee of experts from various industries, showcasing the ability to bring together different perspectives for a common cause.*

The committee played a crucial role in crafting a compelling narrative for lawmakers.

➤ **Inspiration and Leadership:** *Inspiration and leadership provided through a tumultuous journey, offering unwavering guidance during the crisis.*

Ramji became a beacon of leadership, invoking wisdom and stories to motivate the team in challenging times.

➤ **Legacy of Resilience:** *Left a lasting legacy of resilience within Cognos Technologies, showcasing that challenges could be harnessed as opportunities for growth.*

The company emerged from the storm with a strengthened spirit, ready to face future challenges undeterred.

Applying the Dynamic 7G Transcendental Framework

Growth:

Turned the regulatory crisis into an opportunity for the company to evolve and overcome challenges.

Prompted the team to explore growth-oriented solutions rather than succumbing to immediate setbacks through the Socratic approach.

Guidance:

Provided guidance by introducing a Socratic approach, encouraging critical thinking and thoughtful questioning among the leadership team.

Guided the team in aligning their core values with the decisions they were facing in the wake of regulatory challenges.

Grit:

Demonstrated grit by not only acknowledging the severity of the situation but also by inspiring the team to face the regulatory challenges head-on.

Advocated for challenging the regulators, emphasizing that risk is inherent in innovation.

Gallantry:

Displayed gallantry by taking on the regulatory challenges with a determined and courageous approach.

Advocated for fighting for the company's vision, even in the face of potential setbacks, showcasing a brave and resolute stance.

Gratitude:

Instilled a sense of gratitude by appreciating the indomitable spirit and determination within Cognos Technologies.

Recognized the energy and will to thrive, even in the face of adversity, highlighting the essence that made the company exceptional.

Glow:

The implementation of a Socratic approach and the subsequent victory over regulatory challenges brought a glow of success and accomplishment to Cognos Technologies.

The leadership team, under Ramji's guidance, achieved a triumph of innovation over adversity, creating a positive glow within the organization.

Greatness:

Aimed for greatness by positioning Cognos Technologies as not just a company facing regulatory challenges but as a representative of India's tech prowess.

The successful navigation through regulatory hurdles and the subsequent legislative changes contributed to the greatness of the company.

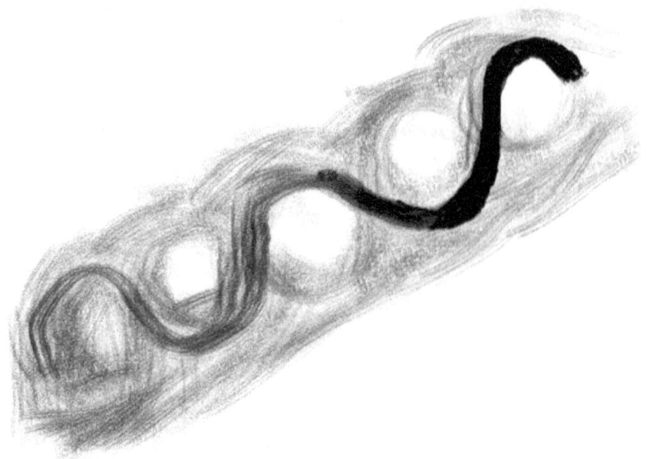

"In the realm of serene symphony, meditation emerges as the maestro, conducting the profound energies latent within. The dance of breath, entwined with the tapestry of stillness, begets a metamorphosis of the mind—a haven of lucidity arising from the tumult of thoughts. Within this tranquil expanse, a transcendental unfoldment transpires; quantum energy personified, navigating boundless vistas within the spectrum of potentialities."

Episode #8:

Eclipsing Ordinary: The Heartfelt Harmony of Wisdom, Meditation, and Professional Metamorphosis

The conference room hummed with eager anticipation as a team of committed professionals convened around the expansive oak table for a session led by Ramji. Keeping the session topic under wraps, Ramji aimed to prevent participants from forming preconceptions. His intent was to encourage everyone to approach the session with an open mind, fostering an atmosphere of curiosity and engagement.

"Ramji," Vishwa began tentatively, "we've always been amazed by your ability to navigate through complex challenges and come up with profound solutions. How do you do it? What's your secret?"

Ramji lounged in his chair, a knowing smile playing on his lips—a silent proclamation of the profound wisdom he bore, and the excitement to reveal it. Sensing the team's heightened curiosity, he opted to unravel a topic that had remained hidden in the folds of anticipation. What unfolded next was a delightful surprise—the very content Ramji had carefully orchestrated for the session!

"My friends," Ramji declared, his voice resonating with the richness of experience, "believe it or not, this was precisely what I had in store for today's session. The essence of my journey lies in the profound influence of meditation—a practice close to my heart, one I wholeheartedly embrace. In a world saturated with information and knowledge, the true depth of wisdom frequently fades into the background."

DIKW Concept - Nurturing Wisdom in the Information Age

He paused for a moment, allowing his words to settle in the room. "You see," he continued, "there's a concept called DIKW—Data, Information, Knowledge, and Wisdom. While data and information are readily available to us, knowledge and wisdom are the treasures that require deep observation, enhancing one's perception skills, and the practice of ancient teachings."

Ramji leaned forward, his eyes gleaming with a profound intensity. "To enhance perception," he explained, "we must first understand the importance of practice. Knowledge is overrated in a world that bombards us with information and distractions. We're often fooled by objects and the hype played by the media, and in the process, we lose connection with the essence of our soul."

Meditation - A Journey Inward to Rediscover Essence

The room fell into a reflective silence as Ramji's words resonated with each team member. He continued, "We all possess a consciousness, a divine spark, that resides within us. Meditation is the bridge that allows us to tap into that infinite well of wisdom. It's a journey inward, a path to rediscover the true part of ourselves that remains unsullied by the noise of the world."

"Within each of us," Ramji continued, "there exists a source of answers and solutions, a connection to the collective consciousness or the divine. True education, my friends, is not about pouring information into the mind but about bringing out that inherent wisdom."

He leaned back again, a serene expression on his face. "Unfortunately, the modern world bombards us with information but neglects the process of true education. We must take time to disconnect from the external chaos and reconnect with the wisdom within." Ramji's gaze softened as he shared a simple yet profound truth. "Meditation," he said, "is not a complicated practice. It's a journey of simplicity and presence. Starting each day with meditation can transform the way we experience life. It enhances our day, sharpens our focus, and heightens our productivity."

Eternal Learning - The Lifelong Student

"I want to delve into another aspect of personal growth—one that has been instrumental in my own journey." He leaned forward, his eyes sparkling with an unquenchable thirst for knowledge. "It's the importance of being a perpetual student, a lifelong learner. You see, life is a grand university, and every experience, every challenge, is an opportunity to embrace lifelong learning."

Ramji's eyes carried a fond reminiscence as he shared, "I've been fortunate to have had several mentors and guides in my life—individuals who have not only imparted knowledge but also shared their wisdom and experiences."

He paused, allowing the significance of his words to resonate. "A coach or guru," Ramji emphasized, "is like a beacon of light in the darkness of ignorance. They guide us, challenge us, and help us unlock our full potential. They offer insights that books and classrooms cannot."

The team members exchanged knowing glances, their own experiences with mentors coming to mind. Ramji's words were a reminder of the power of guidance and mentorship in their personal and professional growth.

"As leaders," Ramji reflected, "we must remain eternal students, always hungry for knowledge and wisdom. And, we must seek the guidance of those who have tread the path before us. It's in this perpetual quest for learning and the wisdom of a guiding light that we truly thrive." As the soft light in the room continued to create an atmosphere of contemplation, Ramji began talking about another important lesson, the team leaned in, eager to absorb the lessons that were about to unfold.

Ancient Wisdom - The Timeless Practice of Apprenticeship

"I want to take you on a journey back in time—an exploration of a practice that dates back to the ancient days of apprenticeship."

He paused, allowing the notion to settle. "In those times," he continued, "the transfer of knowledge and skills was a deeply personal and hands-on process. Masters passed down their expertise to apprentices, not just through words, but through immersive experiences."

The team nodded in understanding. Ramji's words painted vivid scenes of blacksmiths passing down their craft to eager apprentices and wise sages sharing ancient insights with devoted disciples.

Shifting gears, Ramji delved into a captivating facet of human psychology. "Enter the realm of neuroscience," he enlightened, "and encounter the marvel of mirror neurons. These extraordinary brain cells not only enable us to comprehend but also forge an emotional link with the experiences of those around us."

Leaning in with contagious enthusiasm, he continued, "Think of mirror neurons as the interactive bridge connecting teacher and student. When a mentor demonstrates a concept or imparts wisdom, our mirror neurons ignite, forming a profound connection that transcends the limitations of language."

Intrigued glances circulated among the team members, grasping the profound implications of this neurological phenomenon in the context of learning and mentorship.

Without missing a beat, Ramji pressed on, "The significance of staying connected with one's teacher, mentor, or coach cannot be emphasized enough. This unique relationship nourishes our mirror neurons, enabling us to assimilate not just knowledge but the very essence of their wisdom."

To illustrate, he shared a personal anecdote. "In my own odyssey, I've been fortunate to maintain connections with my mentors over the years. Their guidance hasn't merely enriched my understanding; it has kept the flame of wisdom burning within me."

Shifting to a contemplative tone, Ramji emphasized, "In a modern era drowning in knowledge but parched for wisdom, it's imperative that we acknowledge the timeless value of this ancient practice. By staying tethered to our teachers, mentors, and guides, we unlock a reservoir of knowledge and wisdom that transcends generations."

Ramji illuminated the team on the fascinating technical aspect of mirror neurons, a phenomenon firmly grounded in the realm of neuroscience. "Here's the scientific essence," he began, "mirror neurons are validated in the field of neuroscience, and they take center stage in observational learning. When you observe someone in action, your mirror neurons kick in, firing up as if you're personally engaged in the activity. This process fosters a profound empathetic connection, laying the biological foundation for the deep teacher-student relationship I've been highlighting. Essentially, it creates a neurological bridge, facilitating the seamless transfer of knowledge and wisdom."

Devotion in Action - Work as a Spiritual Quest

Ramji continued with a knowing smile, "I've always believed that the best way for me to reach my own depths of the soul is through the work I do." He paused to let the idea sink in. "My work is my prayer. My meditation. My devotion is not about being submissive to someone or something. It's about being dedicated to a cause or a pursuit with deep reverence and love."

The team nodded in understanding, sensing the profound truth in Ramji's words. "I am devoted to my work," Ramji emphasized, "and I believe that I will encounter my highest version through my unwavering dedication to it."

He went on to cite examples of a few individuals who had achieved the highest states of consciousness through their devotion to their work. "Take Nikola Tesla, for instance," Ramji said, his eyes alight with admiration. "His dedication to understanding the mysteries of the universe was nothing short of a spiritual quest. He tapped into realms of knowledge that transcended the material world."

He continued, "Dr. A.P.J. Abdul Kalam, the 'Missile Man of India,' was not just an exceptional scientist but also a true karma Yogi. His dedication to the advancement of technology and science was an expression of his devotion to the betterment of humanity."

Ramji's voice resonated with reverence as he mentioned other luminaries. "Narayana Murthy of Infosys, E. Sreedharan, the 'Metro Man' of India—these are a few examples of individuals who have dedicated themselves to their work with unwavering devotion. They have shown us that through our commitment to our chosen path, we can reach states of consciousness that are truly transformative."

As Ramji concluded his discourse on meditation and devotion to work, the room remained steeped in a profound sense of purpose and inspiration. The understanding that one's work could be a sacred journey—a path to spiritual fulfillment—resonated deeply with each member of the team.

Ramji, their wise mentor, stood before his attentive team, ready to impart his insights on the profound impact of meditation. He began with a warm smile, emphasizing the importance of starting the day with a morning meditation practice.

Morning Meditation - Setting the Tone for the Day

"Embarking on the journey of morning meditation," Ramji proposed, "offers more than a serene start to the day. It's a scientifically backed ritual that intricately influences our biochemistry, setting the stage for heightened productivity and holistic well-being."

Ramji, delving into the technical aspects, elucidated, "As you engage in mindful breathing, a cascade of physiological responses unfolds. Cortisol, the stress hormone, undergoes a decline, fostering a state of tranquility. Simultaneously, neurotransmitters like serotonin surge, enhancing mood and promoting a sense of well-being."

He guided the team through the process, instructing, "Seated comfortably, eyes closed, focus on the breath. As you breathe, pay attention to any subtle sensations or shifts in your body. Feel the gentle rise and fall of your energy, attune yourself to the harmonious rhythms that echo the intricate dance of hormones within. With persistent practice, you not only anchor your mind in the present but also sculpt a neurochemical environment conducive to sustained focus and mental clarity."

In a synchronized breath, Ramji and the team embraced the morning meditation, forging a connection between the rhythm of breath and the orchestration of biochemical balance. "Note the ebb and flow of thoughts," Ramji advised, "and gently steer the mind back to the breath. This cyclical observation and realignment create a robust foundation for mindfulness, fostering resilience throughout the day."

Recognizing the evolving dynamics as the day unfolded, Ramji discerned the accumulating fatigue within his team. Sensing the opportune moment, he introduced them to the rejuvenating practice of afternoon meditation, a strategic intervention to address the demands of a progressing day.

This nuanced approach to meditation, seamlessly weaving into the fabric of the day, showcases not only the spiritual and mental benefits but also the tangible impact on the intricate dance of hormones and neurotransmitters. Ramji's guidance transforms meditation from a ritual into a scientifically informed practice, optimizing the team's vitality and performance.

Afternoon Meditation - A Rejuvenating Elixir

Ramji seamlessly transitioned into the intricate realm of afternoon meditation, unraveling its profound impact on the human brain through the lens of neurobiology. The team, already captivated by his insights, eagerly awaited the revelation of the scientific underpinnings of this transformative practice.

"As the clock gracefully advances past noon, our bodies partake in a ballet of alertness and repose" Ramji began, his voice resonating with a blend of authority and serenity. "This is a consequence of the morning's cognitive exertion, a depletion that necessitates replenishment. It's a harmonious choreography orchestrated by our internal circadian rhythms and the rhythmic dance of neurotransmitters. To grasp this symphony is to navigate its rhythmic poetry. Afternoon meditation emerges as a rejuvenating elixir, precisely tailored to reinvigorate the fatigued mind."

He drew a metaphorical parallel, likening the brain's incessant thinking process to an unending treadmill. "Picture your mind as a relentless runner on this treadmill of thoughts, decisions, and actions. Just like any machinery, it requires a momentary pause, a respite to rest and recharge."

The team nodded in acknowledgment, grasping the analogy of the tireless mind as a perpetual treadmill. Ramji continued, "Afternoon meditation functions as that indispensable pause button. It's a brief yet potent intermission, allowing your mind to step off the treadmill, take a profound breath, and reset."

Expanding on the concept, he articulated, "When you engage in afternoon meditation, you initiate a meaningful pause in your day—a concise yet influential interlude that demarcates the morning's activities from the tasks of the afternoon. This breather acts as a revitalizing intermission for your mind, affording an opportunity to reawaken mental clarity and prepare for the upcoming challenges of the day."

He delved deeper, elucidating, "Granting your brain this respite not only renews cognitive capacities but also taps into reservoirs of creativity and inspiration. It's akin to unlocking a gateway to innovative thinking and unexplored possibilities."

To illustrate this point, Ramji shared a personal anecdote. "Many of my groundbreaking ideas have emerged during afternoon meditation. The stillness of the practice seems to open a portal to a realm of untapped creativity. The practice influences brain wave patterns, creating a canvas of relaxed alertness that counters the post-lunch sluggishness."

Intrigued glances circulated among the team members, captivated by the prospect of harnessing the potential of afternoon meditation for heightened productivity and creativity. Ramji pressed on, "Essentially, when you partake in afternoon meditation, you are essentially living two days in one. The morning is dedicated to focused, task-oriented work, while the afternoon unfolds as an opportunity for a fresh start—a canvas upon which you can paint your creative insights and confront challenges with renewed vigor."

Speaking from personal experience, he emphasized the immense benefits of this practice. Yet, he acknowledged the individuality of the experience, encouraging each team member to discover similar patterns unique to their journey.

Ramji highlighted the ease of weaving afternoon meditation into your daily schedule. "No need for a lengthy session," he recommended. "Just a few minutes of mindful breathing can unlock profound results."

Offering a practical tip, Ramji suggested, "Consider taking a short walk in nature during your lunch break. This simple act of connecting with the natural world serves as a mini-meditation, enabling you to recharge and return to your tasks with a clearer mind."

The room retained a tranquil ambiance, team members absorbing the significance of Ramji's revelations. The legacy of apprenticeship and the magic of mirror neurons had illuminated their understanding of the timeless bond between teacher and student—a bond that continued to shape their journey of wisdom and growth.

Ramji's wisdom flowed seamlessly as he delved into the intricate tapestry of meditation, transforming the room into a sacred space for the exchange of profound insights.

His eyes sparkled with a gentle intensity as he expressed, "Throughout history, various spiritual traditions have devised unique methods to seek the truth, to connect with the divine. Yogis, Sufis, Shamans—they all have their distinctive ways of pursuing the ultimate level of consciousness and oneness with their true nature." The team, attentive and resonant, recognized the universal quest for spiritual connection that transcends cultural and temporal boundaries.

Embarking on the Twilight Meditation Symphony - A Technical Unveiling

Ramji, the virtuoso of mindful rituals, didn't simply bring the day to a close with afternoon meditation; he orchestrated a symphony, introducing the twilight harmony of gratitude meditation. With a rhythmic finesse, he unraveled the technical intricacies, unveiling how this practice, like an alchemical elixir, could intertwine with the threads of our biology and psychology, creating a tapestry of enhanced effectiveness and deeper connections.

"As the celestial curtain descends, inviting the embrace of night, I propose we delve into the final movement of our daily symphony with a session of gratitude meditation," resonated Ramji's voice, a harmonic blend of wisdom and tranquility.

The Neurochemistry of Gratitude - A Symphony in Hormones

"Guiding the team through an enchanting journey into hormone dynamics during gratitude meditation, Ramji encouraged them to envision the canvas of their day. "Observe the captivating ballet of hormones—a graceful choreography that unfolds as you revisit moments filled with gratitude."

He explained how cortisol, the stress hormone, gracefully yielded the stage to oxytocin—the hormone of connection and bonding—during expressions of gratitude. "As you express gratitude, oxytocin surges, weaving threads of connection and fostering a sense of well-being."

In the alchemy of gratitude, serotonin took center stage—a neurotransmitter orchestrating a symphony of positivity. "Each grateful thought becomes a note in this uplifting melody, elevating your emotional and mental resonance."

Ramji elucidated on the role of gratitude in the nocturnal serenade. "As you retire, gratitude meditation becomes a melodic prelude. The act of counting blessings induces a state of calm, coaxing the brain to release melatonin—the conductor of restful slumber."

"Gratitude isn't confined to wakeful moments; it seeps into the realm of the subconscious as you drift into sleep. The neurons dance to the tune of appreciation, entwining gratitude into the very fabric of your being."

Extending the practice beyond individual well-being, he emphasized its cosmic resonance. "Gratitude, a universal language, fosters connection with nature. As you express thanks, you harmonize with the rhythms of the natural world, becoming a note in the grand cosmic cadence."

Professional Success - From Gratitude to Prosperity

The sage of mindful living underscored the connection between gratitude meditation and professional success. "A heart filled with appreciation isn't merely a personal treasure; it's a key to professional prosperity. Gratitude fosters resilience, creativity, and harmonious collaborations—a recipe for success in the professional tapestry."

"In this twilight meditation symphony," Ramji concluded, "gratitude becomes the nocturne that cradles you into the night. As you embrace this practice, you embark on a journey of self-discovery and profound wisdom, weaving a life that resonates with the symphony of a truly well-lived existence."

Quantum Fusion - A Harmonious Ballet of Science and Spirituality

In the contemporary tapestry of existence, a mesmerizing dance unfolds—a convergence where the intricate threads of quantum physics intricately weave into the ancient choreography of meditation. Ramji, the guiding sage of this cosmic symphony, drew parallels between the intricacies of quantum physics and the profound wisdom embedded in meditation, crafting a narrative that resonated with the very essence of the universe.

"As we navigate the realms of quantum physics and meditation," Ramji's voice resonated, "we embark on a journey where energies, both seen and unseen, orchestrate a melody of profound understanding and interconnectedness."

Ramji unveiled the first act of this cosmic ballet, delving into the intricate ballet of quantum particles and their dance within. "In the quantum cosmos, particles engage in instantaneous communication, transcending the constraints of time and space. Similarly, in meditation, neural signals perform a symphony within, traversing the vast landscape of consciousness in a dance of seamless connection."

"As we meditate," Ramji continued, "we attune ourselves to cosmic energies, aligning with the resonances that echo through the quantum fabric. It's not merely a personal journey; it's a cosmic symphony where individual energies harmonize with the universe's majestic cadence."

"Quantum entanglement, the entwining of particles across distances, finds its reflection in emotional alchemy during meditation. The meditator becomes entangled with the cosmic tapestry, transmuting emotions into energies that reverberate with the universal vibrations."

He delved into the quantum ballet of hormones. "Hormones, the quantum messengers of our biology, respond to the vibrations of meditation. Cortisol bows to the quantum signals of serenity, ushering in a cascade of biochemical harmony—a symphony of well-being."

"In meditation, we don't merely connect with our inner self; we tap into the quantum consciousness that permeates the universe," Ramji elucidated. "It's a dance with the cosmic mind, a communion where individual consciousness merges with the vast expanse of quantum awareness."

"The quantum realm teaches us about the power of intention," Ramji declared. "Likewise, in meditation, our intentions become quantum echoes, resonating with the cosmic field. What we manifest in our thoughts transcends into the quantum realm, creating ripples of possibility in the universe."

As Ramji concluded this quantum exploration, the room pulsated with the resonance of newfound wisdom. "In this fusion of quantum wisdom and lifelong learning," he affirmed, "meditation becomes the vessel that sails through the cosmic sea. Empowered by quantum insights, our journey becomes a testament to the symbiosis of science and spirituality, guiding us toward lives brimming with purpose, abundance, and the ineffable wisdom of the cosmos."

Unconventional Leadership Week - A Journey Beyond Norms

The week at Cognos Technologies began just like any other, but a sense of intrigue and curiosity enveloped the leadership team. Ramji, renowned for his unconventional coaching methods, had declared a break from the usual one-on-one meetings. Instead, he had something unexpected and far more immersive in mind.

He gathered the leaders and announced, "This week, I won't be scheduling any formal meetings. I want to truly connect with the rhythm and energy of our company. Every organization has a unique pulse, a living entity of its own, and I aim to tap into it."

The room buzzed with uncertainty and excitement. Ramji was known for his innovative approaches, and this was no exception.

He continued, "I'll be open to offering real-time solutions and being of immediate help in the situations you encounter. No more passing down generic wisdom from a distance."

The leaders exchanged intrigued glances. Ramji's unconventional approach challenged the norms of leadership coaching. "I'll be visiting your departments as an observer rather than a coach," he declared. "I want to immerse myself in the day-to-day experiences, to understand the nuances of our challenges and opportunities firsthand."

The leaders were perplexed but also energized by the prospect. Ramji's decision to step into their world, to feel the pulse of their departments, sparked a sense of anticipation and curiosity. The week ahead promised to be unlike any other, as they wondered what insights Ramji's unconventional approach might reveal and how it could shape the future of their leadership and the company itself.

Takeaways

➤ **DIKW Concept Introduction:** *Understanding the DIKW concept: Data, Information, Knowledge, and Wisdom.*

   Importance of wisdom in the information age.

➤ **Meditation for Wisdom:** *Significance of meditation as a journey inward.*

   Rediscovering one's true essence through meditation.

➤ **Lifelong Learning Advocacy:** *Lifelong learning as a perpetual student.*

   Role of mentors and guides in providing insights.

➤ **Exploration of Ancient Practices:** *Insight into ancient apprenticeship practices.*

Connecting neuroscience, mirror neurons, and hands-on knowledge transfer.

- **Work as a Spiritual Quest:** *Belief in work as a form of devotion.*

  Examples of individuals who dedicated themselves to work as a spiritual quest.

- **Guidance Through Meditation Practices:** *Morning meditation benefits: biochemical impact on stress hormones.*

  Afternoon meditation as a rejuvenating practice for creativity.

- **Gratitude Meditation for Personal and Professional Growth:** *Neurochemistry of gratitude meditation.*

  Professional success through fostering resilience and collaboration.

- **Quantum Fusion of Science and Spirituality:** *Convergence of quantum physics and meditation.*

  Tapping into quantum consciousness through meditation.

- **Unconventional Leadership Week:** *Stepping away from traditional coaching methods.*

  Immersion in day-to-day experiences for a deeper understanding.

Attainments

- **DIKW Concept Integration:** *Successful introduction and understanding of the DIKW concept.*

  Emphasis on the relevance of wisdom in the information age.

- **Meditation Advocacy Impact:** *Effective promotion of meditation as a transformative practice.*

  Team acknowledgment of the journey inward and rediscovery of true essence.

➢ **Lifelong Learning Promotion:** *Successful advocacy for perpetual learning.*

Recognition of the pivotal role of mentors and guides in personal and professional growth.

➢ **Ancient Practices Exploration:** *Team engagement in the exploration of ancient apprenticeship practices.*

Integration of neuroscience and mirror neurons into the understanding of knowledge transfer.

➢ **Spiritual Work Belief Establishment:** *Successful establishment of work as a form of devotion.*

Examples of individuals as inspirations for dedicating work to a higher purpose.

➢ **Effective Meditation Guidance:** *Team adoption of morning meditation for stress reduction.*

Acknowledgment of afternoon meditation's impact on creativity and innovation.

➢ **Gratitude Meditation Influence:** *Team recognition of the neurochemical impact of gratitude meditation.*

Alignment of gratitude practices with personal and professional success.

➢ **Quantum Fusion Acknowledgment:** *Successful communication of parallels between quantum physics and meditation.*

Team understanding of meditation's role in tapping into quantum consciousness.

Applying the Dynamic 7G Transcendental Framework

Growth:

Emphasized continuous growth through lifelong learning, meditation, and devotion to work.

Guidance:

Highlighted the importance of mentors and guides in personal and professional growth.

Encouraged a perpetual quest for knowledge and seeking guidance from experienced individuals.

Grit:

Focused on meditation, devotion to work, and the unconventional leadership week as demonstrations of resilience and determination.

Gallantry:

Emphasized the timeless practice of apprenticeship and mirror neurons as a gallant approach to learning and leadership.

Gratitude:

Incorporated gratitude into the daily routine, linking it to professional success and emphasizing its impact on overall well-being.

Glow:

Presented morning and afternoon meditation practices as ways to enhance well-being, productivity, and mental clarity, contributing to a positive "glow."

Greatness:

Fused quantum physics and meditation, highlighting the potential for greatness by tapping into universal energies and consciousness.

"In the realm of leadership, harmonize the symphony of nurture and restraint. Let the elements converge organically, fostering growth in its natural cadence. Make choices with discernment, avoiding abrupt disruptions. The opus unfolds as a quiet metamorphosis, a ballet of subtle influence, reshaping the tapestry of endeavors."

Episode #9:

Harmony Unveiled: The Culmination of Nature's Symphony

"Don't shout at the Crop for Not Growing fast" - Rohan's Transformation

Rohan, the head of the development team, had been grappling with the weight of a recent project failure. It was a particularly challenging day when Ramji decided to join the daily status meeting of the development team as a spectator, part of the planned leadership week. The room was filled with tension as the team discussed the project's setbacks and the issues they had encountered.

Ramji observed the meeting quietly, taking in the dynamics and the responses of the team members. He noticed Rohan, who appeared visibly frustrated and agitated. The meeting was fraught with tension, with voices raised, and blame cast on various aspects of the project.

As the daily status meeting of the development team began, the atmosphere in the room was tense.

The team members sat around a large conference table, each one with a stern expression, fully aware of the critical nature of the project. Rohan, the head of the development team, was at the head of the table, his face etched with anxiety and frustration.

As the meeting progressed, issues with the project started surfacing.

Delays, technical challenges, and unforeseen obstacles had plagued their progress. Rohan's frustration grew with each problem that was discussed. His tone, initially measured, began to rise as he addressed the team.

"I can't stress enough how crucial this project is," Rohan declared, his voice becoming increasingly emphatic. "We've encountered delays at almost every turn, and it's unacceptable. We need to get this back on track immediately!"

His frustration was palpable, and it didn't take long before the volume of his voice rose considerably. He began pointing out individual team members, questioning their contributions and the reasons for the setbacks. "I need each one of you to step up and take responsibility. This is not a time for excuses; it's a time for action!" Rohan's words were sharp, and his face turned red with frustration. The tension in the room escalated as team members exchanged uncomfortable glances, feeling the weight of Rohan's anger.

The meeting continued in this strained manner, with Rohan's increasingly raised voice reverberating through the room.

Despite his intentions to emphasize the project's importance, it became evident that the team was discouraged and dispirited by his approach.

After the tumultuous status meeting, the atmosphere in the room was heavy with tension. The team members were disheartened and demotivated by Rohan's frustrated outburst. They exchanged uncomfortable glances, acutely aware of the weight of their head's anger. The critical project was in dire straits, and Rohan's approach had not yielded the desired results.

Feeling the weight of disappointment after the tumultuous meeting, Rohan sought solace in Ramji's office. Leaning in, he opened up, "Ramji, today's meeting was a real roller-coaster. This project is hanging in the balance, and I had to crank up the volume to drive home its significance."

Ramji's guidance marked a turning point in Rohan's career. He introduced the farm wisdom principle: "Don't shout at the crops for not growing." Rohan, intrigued, inquired further, "What do you mean by that, Ramji?"

Ramji elaborated, "In essence, Rohan, it means that even in moments of frustration and high stakes, it's more productive to look deeper into the situation. Instead of blaming the team or emphasizing their faults, we should try to identify the underlying issues that might be affecting their performance. It's a more constructive approach to leadership."

He continued, "A farmer doesn't yell at the crops for not growing as expected. Instead, he examines the conditions—whether it's the soil, the water, the nutrients, or other factors —and make necessary adjustments to create an environment where the crops can thrive. Similarly, in leadership, when things go awry, it's more effective to understand the root causes of the issues and work on improving the conditions for success."

Rohan listened intently, realizing the depth of the principle and how it applied to their situation. "So, you're saying I shouldn't have shouted at the team?"

Ramji nodded, offering guidance. "Exactly, Rohan. Leadership is about taking ownership and guiding your team effectively. Instead of pointing fingers when things go south, leaders should ask themselves, 'What can I do better to empower my team to succeed?'"

"Rohan," Ramji started, "I want to emphasize the importance of tonality in your communication. How you convey your message can be as vital as the message itself. Think of it as the music of leadership. It can either create harmony or discord within your team."

Rohan listened attentively, understanding that Ramji was about to provide valuable insights. Ramji continued, "Your tonality in the meeting was rather harsh and agitated, especially during high-stress situations. When your tone is harsh, it can often overshadow the message you're trying to convey. It can make your team defensive, demotivated, and less receptive to your guidance."

Rohan nodded, reflecting on his past behaviour. He admitted, "I can see how my tone might have affected the team negatively. It wasn't my intention, but I realize it came across that way."

Ramji acknowledged Rohan's self-awareness and offered guidance, saying, "Recognizing the issue is the first step towards improvement. In high-stress situations, it's essential to maintain a composed and empathetic tone. Your team should feel supported and motivated by your words, not demoralized. It's a matter of maintaining a balance between urgency and understanding."

He continued, "Effective tonality involves being mindful of your voice's pitch, volume, and rhythm. It should convey your passion and commitment without resorting to aggression or frustration. Think of it as a farmer's approach – a farmer doesn't shout at the crops for them to grow; they nurture the conditions to ensure growth."

Rohan immersed himself in these enlightening revelations, recognizing the profound impact of tonality on effective leadership. Understanding the power of maintaining a calm and empathetic tone, he envisioned fostering a work environment that was not only positive but also highly productive. This pivotal conversation became a catalyst in Rohan's journey of leadership transformation, prompting him to integrate these principles into his daily interactions with the team and witnessing the tangible outcomes unfold.

Don't Uproot the Crop Before They Have a Chance to Grow - Maya's Transformation

Maya had been grappling with a challenging issue in her role as the Head of HR at Cognos Technologies. She entered Ramji's office, looking somewhat uneasy but determined to seek guidance.

After the initial pleasantries, Maya leaned forward, her expression a mix of frustration and concern. "Ramji," she began, "I've been dealing with a recurring problem in our HR department, and I'm not quite sure how to handle it."

Ramji, exuding his trademark tranquility and empathetic demeanor, gently prompted Maya to open up. "Maya, don't hesitate to share any concerns. I'm here to support you." Ramji had keenly observed Maya's leadership style and her interactions with the team throughout this intensive leadership week.

Maya sighed, clearly relieved to have an empathetic ear. "You see, Ramji, we've been actively hiring freshers to infuse new talent into our organization. While many of them show promise, there have been instances where their performance has fallen short of our expectations. Some of our managers are suggesting that we should let go of a few of them."

Ramji nodded, fully comprehending the dilemma. Balancing the need for excellence with nurturing talent was a challenge faced by many organizations.

Maya continued, "I believe in giving people a chance to grow and develop, especially early in their careers. But, at the same time, I understand the importance of efficiency in our department. It's a tough call, Ramji."

Ramji listened attentively, recognizing the complexity of the situation. Then, he began, his voice carrying the weight of wisdom.

"Maya, let me share a principle with you: 'Don't Uproot the Crop Before They Have a Chance to Grow.'"

Maya leaned in, her curiosity piqued. "I'm intrigued, Ramji. Can you explain how that principle applies to our situation?"

Ramji obliged, his tone gentle and informative. "In leadership, there's often a temptation to make swift decisions, like letting go of employees who might not be meeting expectations, especially when they're new to the workforce. However, just as a farmer doesn't uproot a crop before it has had a chance to grow, leaders must provide individuals with time and opportunities to develop and mature in their roles."

Maya considered this principle, realizing its relevance to her situation. She understood that the organization needed to find a balance between nurturing the potential of fresh talent and ensuring departmental efficiency.

Ramji continued, "When dealing with freshers, it's crucial to offer them support, guidance, and training to help them succeed. Sometimes, it takes time for them to fully grasp their roles. By uprooting them prematurely, we risk missing out on their true potential."

Maya's perspective began to shift as she absorbed Ramji's words. She realized that, instead of solely focusing on their current performance, they needed to invest in the development of these freshers, providing them with the chance to grow into valuable assets for the organization.

In the months that followed, Maya brought this principle to life in the HR department. She initiated mentorship programs, identified training needs for upskilling, provided necessary training, and established regular feedback sessions for new hires. Instead of giving up on them, she empowered them with the tools and support to excel.

The results were promising. Many of these freshers started to show significant improvement, feeling motivated and valued by the organization that believed in their potential. Maya's approach not only retained talent but also fostered a culture of growth and development within the HR department.

Maya had learned that, in leadership, patience and investment in individual's growth were essential. Just as a farmer doesn't uproot a crop before it has had a chance to grow, leaders should nurture their team members, especially those in the early stages of their careers, to allow them the opportunity to flourish.

Choose the Best Plants for the Soil

Vishwa, the CEO of Cognos Technologies, faced a daunting dilemma. The pivotal role of Chief Growth Officer needed filling, and he found himself caught in a dilemma between two outstanding candidates—Raj and Puja. With stellar records and qualifications, they were not only colleagues but also directly reported to Vishwa, adding an extra layer of complexity to the decision-making process.

As Vishwa weighed his options, he couldn't help but feel torn. He knew that his decision would have a significant impact on the careers and morale of both Raj and Puja. He was worried that choosing one over the other might result in hurt feelings and a strained team dynamic.

One evening, Vishwa decided to seek guidance from Ramji, a mentor known for providing clarity in even the most complex situations. He scheduled an informal meeting with Ramji and found himself sitting across from the wise mentor.

"Ramji," Vishwa began, "I'm in a tough spot. We have an important position to fill, and Raj and Puja are both exceptional candidates. I can't seem to decide whom to promote. They both report to me and have done great work, and I'm worried that if I choose one, the other will get hurt."

Ramji nodded in understanding. "I see, Vishwa. It's not uncommon to face such a dilemma in leadership. But let me share a principle with you that might help: 'Choose the Best Plants for the Soil.'"

Vishwa furrowed his brow, intrigued by the analogy. "What do you mean by that, Ramji?"

Ramji leaned forward, his eyes carrying the weight of experience. "Vishwa, in leadership, it's essential to choose the best person for the job based on their skills, qualifications, and how well they align with the role and the company's needs. It's not about who is better or great, or who gets hurt, but about what's good for the company."

Vishwa nodded, absorbing the depth of Ramji's insight. "You're right, Ramji. I've been reflecting on how Raj and Puja might react to the promotion dynamics. However, the priority should be what benefits the company most. It's clear in theory, but it gets challenging when you're emotionally invested in the team.

Ramji smiled, pleased that Vishwa was grasping the concept. "Exactly, Vishwa. While it's essential to consider your team's feelings and dynamics, the primary factor should be the individual's suitability for the role and their potential contribution to the company's growth."

Over the next few days, Vishwa carefully evaluated Raj and Puja based on their qualifications, experience, and alignment with the role's requirements. It wasn't an easy decision, but he knew that choosing the best person for the job was in the best interest of the company.

Vishwa made the decision to promote Puja as the Chief Growth Officer. She had the qualifications, experience, and skill set that perfectly aligned with the role's requirements. Puja's promotion was not only a testament to her capabilities but also a clear demonstration of Vishwa's commitment to choosing the best person for the job, in line with Ramji's principle of "Choose the Best Plants for the Soil."

But Vishwa knew the difficult part was communicating the decision to Raj. He invited Raj to his room and mentioned his decision to promote Puja.

"Raj, please understand, this decision is in no way a reflection of your abilities or your unwavering commitment to our team. It's crucial to grasp that what I'm about to share follows the fundamental principle of 'Choosing the Best Plants for the Soil'

We recognize your immense value and the impact you've had within our team. Your capabilities are evident, and this isn't about overlooking them. It's about a specific fit for this particular position at this moment.

I want you to know that your potential here remains strong, and your efforts have not gone unnoticed. There are other opportunities where your skills will be a perfect match, and we'll actively work towards finding those avenues where you can thrive and grow within Cognos Technologies.

"Vishwa," Raj began, "I appreciate your recognition of Puja's abilities, but I can't help feeling disheartened about this decision. I thought I had a real shot at the promotion, and in fact I would admit the thought of resigning has come to my mind."

"Raj," Vishwa revealed, "I want you to know that your skills and contributions are highly valued here. The decision wasn't about whether you're good or not; it was about choosing the best fit for this specific role. I've seen how your strengths lie in a different area."

Raj, puzzled, leaned in, curious about what Vishwa was alluding to.

Vishwa continued, "I've thought deeply about your abilities, and I believe you would be an excellent fit for the role of Chief People's Officer. This role requires someone with a deep understanding of team dynamics, individual strengths, and how to nurture talents. You have a unique capability to connect with people, and I've seen you excel in fostering collaboration within the team."

Vishwa's words began to resonate with Raj. Raj nodded, a sense of hope and renewed enthusiasm washing over him. "Thank you, Vishwa. I appreciate your understanding and the opportunity to work in a role that better suits my strengths. I'm excited about this new direction." With this conversation, Raj's resignation plans were set aside, and he embraced the new role of Chief People's Officer with vigor.

It became evident that, just as different plants thrive in particular soils, individuals flourish in roles that align with their unique strengths and abilities.

The decision to choose the best plants for the soil, instead of comparing or competing with one another, had led to a win-win situation. Both Raj and Puja found roles that suited their strengths, and the organization benefited from their expertise and passion. It was a testament to Vishwa's thoughtful and strategic leadership in nurturing talents within the company and ensuring that each team member could contribute to their full potential.

Irrigate and Fertilize

One sunny afternoon, as the concerns within the team continued to brew, Sourav found it increasingly difficult to ignore the pressing issue of their readiness for the impending cybersecurity challenges. He knew that a proactive approach was needed. With determination in his stride, Sourav decided to seek guidance from

Ramji that leadership week. After all he successfully guided him during the hacking incident. He spotted Ramji in the cafeteria and approached him.

"Ramji," Sourav began, his voice tinged with frustration and concern, "I can't shake this feeling of unease about the team's readiness for the cybersecurity challenges ahead. Despite your invaluable assistance in handling the crisis with Mark, the hacker last month, and his exceptional incident responses, we've encountered another sophisticated phishing attack. We need a more proactive approach. It all started with one unsuspecting team member clicking on a malicious link in an email. The attackers gained access to our systems, and before we knew it, we were grappling with a full-blown cybersecurity crisis."

Ramji listened intently, acknowledging the gravity of the situation. "I see, Sourav. Phishing attacks can be incredibly damaging. What challenges did your team face in handling this incident?"

Sourav continued, "The team struggled to contain the breach swiftly. It was frustrating to see that our team was not as prepared as we should have been".

Ramji nodded, understanding the depth of the challenge. "I can see why you're concerned, Sourav. It's vital to ensure your team is well-prepared to handle such incidents. The 'Irrigate and Fertilize' principle from the farm can certainly help in this situation, the principle is all about proactively nourishing and preparing your team for the challenges they may face. Just like a farmer ensures the soil is well- nourished to yield a bountiful harvest, leaders need to make sure their team has the necessary resources, skills, and knowledge to thrive, especially in areas as critical as cybersecurity."

Sourav nodded, absorbing the wisdom in Ramji's words. "So, you're suggesting that we need to invest in our team's training and preparedness, just like a farmer invests in the soil?"

Ramji smiled, pleased with Sourav's understanding. "Exactly, Sourav. It means conducting regular training, providing access to the latest tools and resources, and making sure your team is well-equipped to handle cybersecurity challenges. You don't wait until a crisis occurs; you prepare your team beforehand so they can handle anything that comes their way."

With this newfound perspective, Sourav set to work. Over the following weeks, he worked closely with the team to identify their specific training needs based on past experiences, including the recent phishing attack. They realized the importance of ongoing periodic training, access to cutting-edge tools, and regular testing to enhance their readiness.

As a united force, they orchestrated dynamic cybersecurity training sessions and immersive workshops. Drawing on the expertise of external luminaries, they not only addressed team concerns but also empowered everyone with the latest knowledge and skills essential for collective organizational defense. Notably, Mark, with his swift grasp of new concepts and hacking prowess, promptly translated insights into impactful implementations.

The team's growing confidence over time equipped them to handle potential cybersecurity challenges more effectively. They implemented improved security protocols and response plans, conducting regular simulations to test their readiness. The atmosphere shifted from unease to proactive preparedness.

Sourav's dedication and the application of the "Irrigate and Fertilize" principle had transformed the team's cybersecurity preparedness. They now felt more empowered, and the cybersecurity concerns that once loomed large had been mitigated through proactive leadership and development efforts. This was a testament to the power of addressing specific challenges while adhering to timeless leadership principles.

Takeaways

➤ **Principle of Farm Wisdom:** "Don't shout at the Crop for Not Growing"

Encouraged the team to adopt a constructive approach during setbacks, emphasizing understanding underlying issues rather than blaming individuals.

➤ **Importance of Tonality:** *Emphasized the importance of tonality in communication.*

Advised Rohan to maintain a composed and empathetic tone, highlighting that effective leadership involves mindful control of pitch, volume, and rhythm.

➤ **Principle of Patience and Growth:** "Don't Uproot the Crop Before They Have a Chance to Grow"

Advised Maya to provide support, guidance, and training to freshers, allowing them time to develop, showcasing the importance of nurturing talent.

➤ **Principle of Choosing the Best Fit:** "Choose the Best Plants for the Soil"

Guided Vishwa to prioritize the individual's suitability for the role over personal dynamics, ensuring the best person for the job was selected.

➤ **Principle of Proactive Leadership:** "Irrigate and Fertilize"

Advised Sourav to proactively nourish and prepare the team for cybersecurity challenges through regular training, access to tools, and ongoing skill development.

Achievements

➤ **Shift in Leadership Perspective:** *Enabled the team to handle setbacks more constructively, fostering a positive and growth-oriented mindset.*

- ➤ **Improved Communication Dynamics:** *Guided Rohan in refining his tonality, transforming communication to be more supportive and motivating.*

- ➤ **Enhanced Talent Development:** *Inspired Maya to invest in the growth of freshers, fostering a culture of development within the HR department.*

- ➤ **Strategic Decision-Making:** *Assisted Vishwa in making a decision based on the principle of choosing the best fit for organizational growth.*

- ➤ **Proactive Cybersecurity Leadership:** *Enabled Sourav to lead the team proactively in addressing cybersecurity challenges, transforming concerns into a prepared and confident team.*

Applying the Dynamic 7G Transcendental Framework

Growth:

Encouraged a growth-oriented mindset by emphasizing learning from setbacks and investing in the development of team members.

Guidance:

Provided guidance to individuals like Rohan, Maya, Vishwa, and Sourav, steering them toward effective leadership principles.

Grit:

Demonstrated the importance of perseverance, resilience, and determination in overcoming challenges and achieving success in leadership roles.

Gallantry:

Displayed courage in challenging conventional approaches, advocating for a more constructive and growth-oriented mindset.

Gratitude:

Showcased gratitude toward team members by investing in their growth and development.

Glow:

Advocated for maintaining a positive and motivating tonality, creating harmony within the team.

Greatness:

Encouraged strategic decision-making that aligns with the organization's growth, fostering a culture of greatness.

"Beyond numerical confines, elevate wealth through the interwoven threads of value, service, and prosperity. Immerse in real-time success and strategic guidance. Observe the transformative magic of customer-centric innovation, intertwining with the cultivation of organizational value through a steadfast commitment to the well-being of employees."

Episode #10:

The ProsperaVision Framework:
Elevating Wealth Beyond
Numbers

The boardroom filled with shareholders resonated with the weight of Q1 results, an undeniable tension hanging thick in the air. The CEO of the Big 4 audit firm, a staunch advocate for a purely financial perspective, disdainfully dismissed elements beyond profit and loss, reducing vision, mission, and employee engagement to mere fluff.

"You know, Vishwa, I really think you are wasting your money on this constant pursuit of airy concepts like team building, cohesion, values, and mission. It's all fluff. In business, only profit matters. Emotions, friendships, or bonding – they don't play a role in the cutthroat world of business. I see that you have hired a consultant for this…"

Vishwa, feeling the weight of the critique, squared his shoulders and responded with measured determination, "Profit is undeniably crucial, but our organization is built on more than just financial transactions. The values we uphold, the relationships we foster, and the mission we pursue are integral to our success. They shape our identity and influence how we navigate challenges."

The executives, caught in the crossfire of conflicting perspectives, exchanged uneasy glances, unsure of how the clash between financial orthodoxy and a more holistic approach would unfold.

The auditor dismissed, "A framework won't alter the fact that business revolves around profits and the bottom line, not some abstract ideas."

Vishwa responded, "Yes, we've brought in a consultant. Someone who can help us bridge the gap between the numbers and the essence of our organization. We need a broader perspective to weather the storms ahead. In fact, I believe our productivity has quadrupled, and we made decisions that will have a multiplier effect on our profits because we have Ramji's Framework to guide us in tune with our Mission and Vision than short-term tactical advantages."

With a tone of skepticism, the auditor continued, "You can invest in all the 'holistic' approaches you want, but when it comes down to it, profit is the only language that matters in the business world."

As the tension reached its peak, the team broke for lunch. Vishwa was determined to bring a new perspective into the room and excused himself for the team lunch. In the corridor outside, he picked up the phone and dialed Ramji.

"Ramji, we're at a critical juncture. The auditor, he… he's not seeing beyond profit. The shareholders are hanging on his every word. If we don't impress upon him the value of your framework, our investments will be questioned, and it might cast doubt on our strategic decisions."

Vishwa continued, "I need you to come in and explain to him – show him the financial impact, make him understand that this framework isn't just about ideals, but it's about real, tangible results."

Ramji: "Vishwa, I'm here to help. Let me come in and present a perspective that goes beyond the conventional bottom line. I will be right there for the post-lunch session."

Crisis at the Boardroom

As they walked back into the boardroom, Vishwa leading the way, the tension inside seemed to have escalated. The executives exchanged anxious glances, uncertain of what would unfold next.

Vishwa, addressing the room, announced, "Gentlemen, we have Ramji with us, and he's here to shed light, in fact, he also has a financial framework capturing the true wealth of the organization. Let's give him the floor."

The auditor, still skeptical, raised an eyebrow. "I hope this isn't another distraction."

Vishwa, with a determined gaze, replied, "No, this is an opportunity for us to showcase the true potential of our organization."

Ramji stepped forward, his calm presence commanding attention. "Gentlemen, let's address the misconception that money is merely currency. If it were that simple, governments could print money endlessly, and we'd all be rich. However, history tells a different story. True wealth, my friends, lies in the creation of goods and services."

He continued, "Money is not just a piece of paper; it's a representation of the value we provide to others. It's generated when we address the needs, desires, wants, and aspirations of our customers. It's a byproduct of our ability to serve."

Ramji gestured towards the examples of economic crises in Zimbabwe and Venezuela. "The economies of both countries collapsed when goods and services are not created but money was printed. Everybody has paper money or currency, but they are unable to buy anything because the ability to produce goods or services has not been in proportion to printing money, so let's understand the aspects of money in a deeper way."

"True wealth is born from our ability to serve customers, addressing their needs, desires, and aspirations." Ramji paused, allowing the weight of his words to settle in the room. "Now, I present to you

The ProsperaVision Framework: Elevating Wealth Beyond Numbers

It's not just a set of principles; it's a guide to understanding the intricate dance between value, service, and prosperity. In the interest of time, I'll touch on the key pillars, but the real depth is waiting for you in my upcoming workshops."

Leaning in, Ramji unveiled his framework. "The framework is structured into 5 key pillars, each designed to contribute to the overall success and prosperity of the organization."

He started highlighting the pillars.

Holistic Wealth Understanding - Illuminating the Corporate Tapestry

- This pillar serves as the foundation, emphasizing the journey of enlightenment beyond traditional financial perspectives.

- It encourages a profound understanding of wealth that goes beyond mere numerical values.

- The interwoven threads of value, service, and prosperity create a paradigm shift, where success is measured by the holistic impact on various aspects of the organization.

Hands-On Prosperity - Crafting Success in Real-Time

- This pillar introduces a practical and immersive approach to applying theoretical knowledge.

- Through hands-on exercises and compelling case studies, it transforms abstract concepts into actionable strategies.

➢ It acts as a blueprint for crafting tangible success stories, fostering a culture where theoretical understanding translates into real-world achievements resonating throughout the organization.

Strategic Long-Term Guidance - Navigating the Success Odyssey

➢ This pillar provides strategic guidance for charting a course towards sustainable growth.

➢ Aligned with the organization's mission and values, this pillar acts as a compass for making decisions and taking steps calibrated to ensure enduring success.

➢ The emphasis is on propelling the corporate-ship towards a future where prosperity is not transient but everlasting.

Customer-Centric Alchemy - Innovate, Captivate, Elevate

➢ Positioned as the heartbeat of success, this pillar focuses on innovation to meet and exceed customer needs.

➢ It encourages exploring novel ways to foster lasting relationships with customers, painting a masterpiece of customer-centricity.

➢ Each innovation becomes a brushstroke, positively reverberating through the bottom line and contributing to the overall success narrative.

Employee Well-being Nexus - Cultivating the Seeds of Organizational Value

➢ Recognizing employees as the cornerstone of organizational value, this pillar emphasizes commitment to their well-being.

➢ It guides organizations to enhance employee engagement, foster a culture of well-being, and acknowledge the profound impact employees have on the organizational tapestry of success.

Radiating positivity and confidence, he asserted, "Witness the fusion of holistic wealth understanding, hands-on prosperity, strategic guidance, customer-centric alchemy, and employee well-being, crafting a masterpiece of enduring wealth in the corporate landscape. It's not merely a framework; it's your pathway to a legacy of prosperity beyond measure."

Intrigued by Ramji's holistic approach, the auditor hesitated for a moment before expressing his admiration, "I am truly impressed by your profound understanding of finance, which transcends mere numbers. I look forward to learning from your framework."

With those words, the atmosphere in the room underwent a notable shift. Ramji's invitation not only bridged the gap but also unlocked a door to a profound comprehension of wealth. The boardroom, previously marked by division, was now standing at the threshold of a transformative journey.

Takeaways

> **Holistic Wealth Understanding Pillar:** *Emphasized the creation of goods and services as the true source of wealth.*

> *Introduced the idea that money is a representation of value provided to customers.*

> *Highlighted the importance of understanding wealth beyond numerical values.*

> **Hands-On Prosperity Pillar:** *Advocated for a practical and immersive approach to applying theoretical knowledge.*

> *Transformed abstract concepts into actionable strategies through hands-on exercises.*

Encouraged a culture where theoretical understanding translates into real-world achievements.

> **Strategic Long-Term Guidance Pillar:** *Provided strategic guidance for sustainable growth.*

Aligned the framework with the organization's mission and values.

Acted as a compass for making decisions calibrated for enduring success.

> **Customer-Centric Alchemy Pillar:** *Focused on innovation to meet and exceed customer needs.*

Encouraged novel ways to foster lasting relationships with customers.

Demonstrated how innovation positively impacts the bottom line and contributes to success.

> **Employee Well-being Nexus Pillar:** *Recognized employees as the cornerstone of organizational value.*

Emphasized commitment to employee well-being and engagement.

Acknowledged the profound impact employees have on the organizational tapestry of success.

Attainments

> **Transformation of Perspective:** *Transformed the boardroom atmosphere from skepticism and division to admiration and potential.*

> **Introduction of ProsperaVision Framework:** *Introduced a comprehensive framework that goes beyond conventional financial perspectives.*

Positioned the framework as a guide to understanding the intricate dance between value, service, and prosperity.

➢ **Alignment with Mission and Vision:** *Aligned the framework with the organization's mission and values, emphasizing a broader perspective.*

➢ **Shifted Perception on Wealth:** *Shifted the perception of wealth from a purely financial standpoint to a more holistic understanding.*

Demonstrated the connection between goods, services, and the true essence of money.

➢ **Cultural Shift:** *Initiated a cultural shift where the focus is on enduring success, innovation, and employee well-being.*

Fostered a mindset where prosperity is not transient but everlasting.

Applying the Dynamic 7G Transcendental Framework

Growth:

Encouraged growth through a holistic understanding of wealth and practical application of knowledge.

Guidance:

Provided strategic guidance for long-term success and introduced a framework for practical application.

Grit:

Displayed determination in presenting a holistic framework despite skepticism from the financial advocate.

Gallantry:

Challenged the conventional belief that profit is the only language that matters in business.

Stood firm in presenting a comprehensive framework in the face of criticism.

Gratitude:

Acknowledgement of the thought that contribution of goods and services to the creation of true wealth.

Glow:

Radiated positivity and confidence while presenting the ProsperaVision Framework.

Shifted the atmosphere in the room from division to transformative potential.

Greatness:

Presented a framework as a pathway to a legacy of prosperity beyond measure.

Bridged the gap between financial orthodoxy and a holistic approach, unlocking a transformative journey.

"In the crucible of chaos, the 7G Transcendental Framework emerges as a guiding beacon. With Growth as the compass, Guidance as the anchor, and Grit as the shield, the team navigates the storm, embodying the principles of Gallantry, Gratification, Glow, and ultimately achieving Greatness."

Episode #11:

Igniting Brilliance: Ramji's Revelation of the 7G Transcendental Framework

With the highly anticipated Virtual Gaming Platform Launch jin about 2 months, Ramji approached Vishwa with an intriguing proposition – the application of his transformative 7G Framework to ensure an even more successful launch. Vishwa, fueled by curiosity and eagerness, enthusiastically welcomed the opportunity to delve into the depths of Ramji's renowned framework.

Ramji brought together all the teams for a session where he not only unveiled his potent 7G Transcendental Framework but also demonstrated how the implementation of the 7G framework in various scenarios empowered Cognos to successfully navigate challenges.

Pledging to reveal the essence of each 'G' daily, he assured the teams of profound insights poised to seamlessly integrate into both their personal and professional journeys. He declared that the exploration would begin with the first 'G' of the 7Gs starting from the next day.

Day 1 - Growth: Nurturing Scalability

In the realm of launching a global online gaming platform, Ramji, drawing upon his profound professional acumen and the guiding principles of the 7G Transcendental Framework, channels the energy of the root chakra to tackle the formidable challenge of scalability. This day, marked by the quest for a robust and expansive foundation, becomes a testament to Ramji's strategic prowess.

In the early hours of the day, Ramji assembles his team for the 'big room' event, setting the stage for a profound journey into the Growth principle. With the resilience of the root chakra, symbolizing stability and grounding, Ramji articulates the criticality of scalability in the face of an impending surge in users.

Navigating the Digital Landscape

Ramji, drawing on his wealth of professional experience, charts a meticulous plan to fortify the platform against the impending storm of users. Like the roots of a mighty tree delving deep into the earth, he delves into the intricacies of the powerful server infrastructure, recognizing it as the lifeblood that nourishes the entire gaming ecosystem.

Investing in Stability

Rooted in the essence of the root chakra, Ramji directs strategic investments into a state-of-the-art server infrastructure. It is not merely an allocation of resources; it is a profound act of nurturing the very foundation on which the gaming community will stand. Load testing becomes the crucible through which the servers are tempered, ensuring they can withstand the weight of millions of eager users.

Aligning with Stability

As a seasoned leader, Ramji knows that aligning the team with the Growth principle requires more than just directives—it demands a shared understanding and commitment. Drawing on the grounding force of the root chakra, he instills a collective awareness of the significance of scalability. Each team member becomes a guardian of stability, their roots intertwining to create a network of strength.

The Root Chakra's Resilient Energy

Ramji, channeling the resilient energy of the root chakra, becomes the anchor that steadies the ship. His leadership becomes a force that emanates stability, assuring the team that, no matter the magnitude of the challenge, they stand on a solid foundation.

The Promise of Growth

As the day concludes, Ramji doesn't just leave his team with a scalable platform; he leaves them with a promise of growth. The root chakra's energy, coursing through every decision and investment, becomes a testament to his unwavering commitment to the team's journey into the digital wilderness.

And so, on this day of Growth, Ramji, fueled by professional acumen and transcendental wisdom, paves the way for a gaming platform that not only withstands the surge of users but beckons them into an immersive and stable gaming experience.

Day 2 - Guidance: Crafting a UX Symphony with Sacral Brilliance

Ramji, drawing from the fount of his professional prowess and the vibrant energy of the Sacral Chakra, turns his attention to the challenge of User Experience (UX) Design. The Sacral Chakra, with its creative brilliance, becomes the guiding force as Ramji orchestrates a symphony of design, weaving intuitive interfaces and emotional intelligence into the fabric of the gaming experience.

Amidst the digital canvas, Ramji, attuned to the harmonizing energy of the Sacral Chakra, embarks on a journey to transform the challenge of UX design into an artistic masterpiece that resonates with every user.

Professional Artistry in UX

Ramji, as the maestro of this digital composition, leverages his professional artistry to discern the nuances of UX design. The Sacral Chakra's creative energy infuses every decision, turning the challenge into an opportunity to craft an interface that transcends the features and functionalities of the virtual gaming platform, becoming an immersive piece of interactive art.

Sacral Chakra's Creative Guidance

Guided by the principle of Guidance and fueled by the Sacral Chakra's creative brilliance, Ramji steers the team towards innovative solutions. The Chakra's energy becomes a compass, directing them to design choices that go beyond convention, transforming the user interface into an intuitive playground where users seamlessly navigate.

Collaborative Design Symphony

Riding on the waves of creative energy, Ramji fosters collaboration within the team. Like a conductor unifying diverse instruments, he ensures each team member contributes their unique notes to the UX symphony. The Sacral Chakra's collaborative spirit transforms the design process into a harmonious collaboration, resulting in an interface that resonates with unity.

Emotional Intelligence as Design Elegance

Incorporating the Sacral Chakra's emotional intelligence, Ramji guides the team to infuse the UX design with empathy and understanding. They delve into the emotional landscape of gamers, crafting an interface that not only functions seamlessly but also connects with the users on a profound level. The result is not just a platform; it's an emotional journey for every gamer.

Intuition as the Design Guru

The Sacral Chakra, with its intuitive prowess, becomes the design guru under Ramji's guidance. He encourages the team to trust their instincts, fostering an environment where intuitive design choices flourish. The UX design, shaped by the team's collective intuition, becomes a testament to the power of Sacral wisdom in the digital realm.

Thus, on this day of Guidance, Ramji, attuned to the creative energies of the Sacral Chakra, transforms the challenge of UX design into a digital masterpiece that not only guarantees an intuitive interface but also elevates the gaming experience to an unparalleled realm of artistic brilliance.

Day 3 - Grit: Triumph Over Technical Turbulence with Solar Resilience

As the countdown to the global launch of the virtual gaming platform intensifies, Ramji, drawing from the depths of his professional acumen and the radiant energy of the Solar Plexus Chakra, confronts the formidable challenge of technical glitches. With a heart pulsating with determination and guided by the Solar Plexus Chakra's unwavering strength, Ramji rallies the team to not just face but conquer the looming storm of unexpected technical issues.

In the crucible of Solar energy, Ramji transforms the challenge of technical glitches into an opportunity for the team to showcase resilience, adaptability, and unwavering determination.

Anticipation through Testing

Guided by the Solar Plexus Chakra's foresight, Ramji leads the team in comprehensive testing. Their approach is not just to identify glitches but to anticipate them. The Solar energy infuses the testing process with a proactive mindset, ensuring that potential issues are unearthed and resolved before they can manifest during the grand launch.

Contingency Plans with Solar Precision

Ramji, fueled by the Solar Plexus Chakra's precision, oversees the development of meticulous contingency plans. The Solar energy becomes the beacon that guides the team in crafting strategies to navigate through unexpected technical challenges. Each plan is infused with resilience, ensuring that the team can adapt swiftly to any unforeseen circumstance.

Fostering Solar Resilience

With the Solar Plexus Chakra as the source of inner strength, Ramji encourages the team to embrace resilience as a core value. They engage in workshops and exercises that fortify their mindset, instilling a sense of unwavering determination to face challenges head-on. The Solar energy becomes a force, empowering the team to withstand any turbulence.

Real-Time Adaptability

As the day of the grand launch approaches, Ramji, attuned to the Solar energy, fosters a culture of real-time adaptability within the team. They understand that the digital landscape is dynamic, and glitches may emerge unexpectedly. The Solar Plexus Chakra's energy becomes the driving force, ensuring that the team can adapt swiftly and decisively in the face of unforeseen challenges with unwavering determination, transforming each challenge into a golden opportunity to showcase their collective strength.

A Launch of Solar Brilliance

As the virtual gaming platform prepares for its global debut, the brilliance of the Solar Plexus Chakra illuminates the path forward.

Crafted under Ramji's expert guidance, meticulous testing, strategic contingency plans, and a resilient mindset stand as the bedrock for a flawless launch on the much-anticipated day. The team, fueled by the empowering Solar energy, eagerly envisions triumphing over any technical challenges that may arise.

Looking ahead to the launch, just two months away, Ramji draws strength from the radiant energy of the Solar Plexus Chakra. His vision is clear: turning the imminent technical challenges into a testament of triumph. The launch, transcending a mere showcase of technological prowess, becomes a living embodiment of the team's unwavering determination and resilience in the face of adversity. This future day of Grit promises not just success but a remarkable achievement etched in the team's collective journey.

Day 4 - Gallantry: Upholding Ethical Eminence with the Heart's Integrity

Ramji, drawing from the reservoirs of his professional wisdom and the nurturing energy of the Heart Chakra, confronts the challenge of ensuring ethical gaming practices. The heartbeat of integrity becomes the guiding force as Ramji, with unwavering dedication, leads the team in embracing a culture of gallantry.

Professional Integrity

Ramji, a promoter of professional ethics, recognizes the paramount importance of ethical gaming practices. The Heart Chakra's benevolent energy infuses him with a deep sense of responsibility. With a commitment to transparency and fairness, he embarks on a journey to integrate ethical standards seamlessly into the gaming platform.

Comprehensive Review with Heart's Insight

Empowered by the Heart Chakra's profound insights, Ramji embarks on a thorough examination of gaming practices. The Heart's energy serves as the guiding light, revealing and resolving potential ethical concerns. United under Ramji's compassionate leadership, the team actively participates in open discussions to guarantee that every facet of the platform aligns with the core principles of fairness and integrity, covering aspects like money transactions, offers, discounts, coupons, gifts, and rewards.

Addressing Concerns with Compassion

With the Heart Chakra as the wellspring of compassion, Ramji guides the team in proactively addressing potential concerns. Each decision is carefully weighed, considering its impact on the gaming community. The Heart's energy creates a nurturing environment where concerns are met with genuine empathy, and solutions are forged with a sincere dedication to the users' well-being. Customer success transcends merely resolving challenges; it's approached with heartful compassion and understanding.

Transparency as the Heartbeat

As the team progresses, Ramji, attuned to the Heart Chakra's emphasis on transparency, ensures that every process is open and honest. Users are given insight into the platform's ethical framework, fostering trust and camaraderie. The Heart's energy becomes the heartbeat of transparency, resonating throughout the gaming community.

Educational Initiatives with Heart-Centered Wisdom

Ramji, acknowledging the transformative power of education, launches comprehensive programs aimed at enlightening the gaming community about ethical practices. Guided by the wisdom of the Heart Chakra, these initiatives aim to create an environment where users not only savor the gaming experience but also grasp the significance of ethical conduct within the virtual realm.

In the face of certain unethical behaviors observed in virtual gaming, such as exploiting loopholes for unfair advantages, engaging in cheating practices, or participating in cyberbullying, it becomes imperative to ensure that users are well-informed and discouraged from participating in such activities. Ramji envisions a community that upholds values of fairness, integrity, and respect, fostering an environment where every player contributes to a positive and enriching gaming atmosphere. Through targeted educational campaigns, Cognos must empower users with the knowledge to make ethical choices, promoting a gaming culture built on principles of fairness and sportsmanship.

Heart-Centered Legacy

As the day of Gallantry unfolds, Ramji, driven by the boundless love and integrity of the Heart Chakra, is set to carve out a lasting legacy. The gaming platform, immersed in the nurturing energy of the Heart, is destined to transcend its role as a mere virtual entertainment space. Instead, it will serve as a powerful testament to the transformative impact of ethical conduct. Ramji, the promoter of the Heart's integrity, is dedicated to ensuring that the platform's legacy resonates in the hearts of millions, fostering a community thriving on the principles of fairness, love, and ethical gallantry.

Day 5 - Gratification: Orchestrating Pre-Launch Harmony with Throat Chakra's Clarity

As the virtual gaming platform, eagerly awaited by millions, is getting ready for the launch, Ramji, empowered by both professional expertise and the resonating energy of the Throat Chakra, encounters a multitude of challenges. This day of Gratification becomes a pivotal moment in the pre-launch phase, where Ramji, the harbinger of clarity, weaves a narrative of anticipation, resilience, and community engagement.

Articulating Pre-Launch Vision

Ramji, drawing upon his wealth of professional experience, recognizes the need for a clear articulation of the platform's pre-launch vision. The Throat Chakra's clarity becomes the guiding force as he communicates the team's goals, strategies, and the immersive experience that awaits the gaming community. This transparent articulation sets the stage for Gratification, creating excitement and anticipation among the users before the platform's unveiling.

Building Community Resonance

In the pre-launch phase, the challenge lies in building community resonance without a tangible product. Ramji, attuned to the Throat Chakra's energy, encourages the team to engage with the gaming community through transparent communication. By sharing glimpses of the platform's development process, achievements, and challenges, the team fosters a sense of inclusion and excitement, laying the foundation for a gratifying post-launch experience.

Cultivating a Culture of Appreciation

The Throat Chakra's emphasis on gratitude becomes a cornerstone in the pre-launch preparations. Ramji instills a culture of appreciation within the team, ensuring that every milestone, regardless of scale, is acknowledged and celebrated. This practice not only boosts team morale but sets the tone for post-launch engagement, where the gaming community will be integral to the platform's success.

Anticipating and Mitigating Pre-Launch Challenges

Under the influence of Gratification, Ramji leads the team in anticipating and mitigating pre-launch challenges. Whether it's addressing technical intricacies, refining user interfaces, or preparing for potential social media crises, the Throat Chakra's clarity enables Ramji to navigate these challenges with transparency. By openly communicating the team's strategies for overcoming hurdles, he builds trust among the gaming community, assuring them that their experience is a top priority.

Interactive Pre-Launch Engagement

Embracing the Throat Chakra's love for connection, Ramji leads an engaging pre-launch initiative across social media and various channels. The team actively encourages user participation, attentively gathers expectations, and integrates valuable feedback into the final development stages. This includes thorough beta testing, refining the platform and fostering a pre-launch bond with the gaming community. This paves the way for a post-launch experience that promises mutual satisfaction and enjoyment.

Throat Chakra's Legacy of Clear Resonance

As the day of Gratification unfolds in the pre-launch phase, Ramji, propelled by the Throat Chakra's clarity, leaves behind a legacy of clear resonance. The virtual gaming platform, though yet to be unveiled, becomes a testament to the transformative power of transparent communication and community engagement. Ramji, as the influencer of the Throat's clarity, ensures that the platform's voice echoes with authenticity, gratitude, and a harmonious connection between the creators and the community. This legacy sets the stage for a post-launch era where the gaming community, having been an integral part of the platform's journey, is primed for a gratifying and enduring connection.

Day 6 - Glow: Illuminating Global Collaboration with the Third Eye's Vision

Ramji, wielding both professional acumen and the illuminating energy of the Third Eye chakra, faces the formidable challenge of facilitating effective collaboration across diverse teams, vendors, partners and time zones. Day 6, under the influence of Glow, becomes a beacon of insight and harmonious global engagement.

Harnessing Professional Insight

Guided by the wisdom of the Third Eye chakra, Ramji taps into his professional insight to understand the nuances of global collaboration. Drawing from his wealth of experience, he identifies potential challenges stemming from cultural differences, communication barriers, and varying work methodologies. This foresight allows him to lay the groundwork for a collaborative environment that transcends geographical boundaries.

Cultivating a Positive Mindset

The Third Eye chakra's influence propels Ramji to foster a positive mindset within the team. Recognizing that effective global collaboration requires a collective attitude of openness and adaptability, he encourages team members to embrace diverse perspectives and cultural nuances. By infusing positivity into virtual interactions, Ramji creates an atmosphere where creativity flourishes, and challenges transform into opportunities for growth.

Utilizing Transcendental Vision

Beyond the realms of traditional problem-solving, Ramji, attuned to the Third Eye's transcendental energy, employs a holistic approach to global collaboration. He encourages the team to tap into their intuitive faculties, fostering a deeper understanding of each other's strengths and potential challenges. This transcendental vision allows for a harmonious blending of skills, ensuring that the collective intelligence of the global team is harnessed effectively.

Embracing Virtual Communication Tools

In the era of virtual collaboration, the Third Eye chakra guides Ramji in selecting and implementing communication tools that transcend physical distances. Whether through video conferencing, collaborative platforms, or real-time messaging, he ensures that the chosen tools facilitate seamless interaction, creating a virtual space where ideas flow freely, and the global teams, vendors, and partners operate as one cohesive unit.

Navigating Time Zone Challenges

Understanding the temporal complexities of global collaboration, Ramji, guided by the Third Eye's awareness, devises strategies to navigate time zone challenges. He establishes clear communication protocols, schedules overlapping work hours for critical discussions, and encourages asynchronous collaboration when necessary. This mindful approach ensures that every member of the teams, vendors, and partners regardless of their location, feels valued and included in the collective journey.

Illuminating the Path of Global Unity

As Day 6 unfolds, guided by Glow and the Third Eye chakra's illumination, Ramji leaves an indelible mark on the platform's journey. The challenges of global collaboration, once daunting, transform into opportunities for unity and innovation. The virtual gaming platform, primed for a global launch, stands as a testament to Ramji's ability to harness both professional expertise and the transcendental energy of the Third Eye, creating a harmonious symphony of talents that resonates across continents.

Day 7 - Greatness: Ascending to Market Leadership with the Crown's Radiance

As the grand finale unfolds, Ramji, guided by the principle of Greatness, faces the monumental challenge of establishing the virtual gaming platform as a standout contender in the fiercely competitive gaming market. Harnessing the radiance of the Crown chakra, he weaves together a tapestry of strategies that transcends conventional approaches, ensuring not just success but a lasting legacy in the gaming industry.

Channeling Professional Wisdom

Under the influence of the Crown chakra, Ramji taps into his profound reservoir of professional wisdom. With an understanding of market dynamics, consumer behavior, and emerging trends, he envisions a strategic roadmap for the gaming platform's ascent to greatness. His transcendent perspective allows him to identify gaps in the market and position the platform as a pioneer rather than a follower.

Aligning with Transcendental Purpose

The Crown chakra's energy propels Ramji to align the team with a higher purpose beyond immediate success. He fosters a collective understanding of the platform's mission, emphasizing the positive impact it can have on the gaming community and beyond. This shared transcendental purpose becomes the driving force behind every decision, imbuing the team with a sense of responsibility and passion for creating something truly remarkable.

Innovative Features

Guided by the Crown's radiance, Ramji spearheads the integration of innovative features that set the platform apart. These transcendental enhancements go beyond meeting user expectations, offering a unique and unparalleled gaming experience. Whether through cutting-edge technology, immersive storytelling, or revolutionary gameplay mechanics, the platform must emerge as a beacon of innovation in the gaming landscape.

Holistic Marketing Campaigns

The Crown chakra's influence extends to the realm of marketing, where Ramji orchestrates holistic campaigns that transcend traditional boundaries. Beyond conventional advertising, he leverages the power of storytelling, emotional connection, and community engagement. These campaigns not only promote the platform but also create a narrative that resonates with the audience, fostering a sense of belonging and anticipation.

Sustainable Long-Term Vision

Bathed in the radiance of the Crown Chakra's wisdom, Ramji envisions a strategy for enduring success. Steering clear of short-term gains, he directs the team towards building a legacy that stands resilient against market fluctuations. Infusing the team with a spirit of endurance and adaptability, Ramji ensures that the platform not only survives but thrives in the ever-changing landscape of the gaming industry. Emphasizing the importance of staying abreast of dynamic technology trends, especially in hardware, he envisions seamless integration with the virtual gaming platform, ensuring an unparalleled user experience.

Transcending Boundaries with the Crown's Brilliance

As Day 7 unfolds, culminating in the principle of Greatness, Ramji, guided by the radiance of the Crown chakra, envisions the extraordinary. The virtual gaming platform, once a mere concept, is now on the verge of transforming into a paragon of excellence, innovation, and community. Ramji's skillful navigation of market competition goes beyond conventional strategies, positioning the platform not just as a contender but as a luminary in the gaming cosmos. In the unfolding tapestry of the gaming industry, the brilliance of the Crown chakra illuminates the platform's imminent ascent to greatness.

Takeaways

> **Root Chakra - Day 1 - Growth: Nurturing Scalability:**

Significance of scalability in launching a global online gaming platform.

Utilization of the root chakra's energy for stability and grounding.

Importance of strategic investments in server infrastructure.

> **Sacral Chakra - Day 2 - Guidance: Crafting a UX Symphony:**

Integration of the sacral chakra's creative brilliance in UX design.

Collaborative and intuitive design choices guided by the sacral chakra.

Incorporation of emotional intelligence into the UX design process.

> **Solar Plexus Chakra - Day 3 - Grit: Triumph Over Technical Turbulence:**

Importance of addressing technical glitches with resilience.

Anticipation of challenges through comprehensive testing.

Fostering a culture of real-time adaptability and a triumphant mindset.

> **Heart Chakra - Day 4 - Gallantry: Upholding Ethical Eminence:**

Recognition of the importance of ethical gaming practices.

Comprehensive review of gaming practices guided by the heart chakra.

Commitment to fairness, transparency, and cultivating a culture of appreciation.

➢ **Throat Chakra - Day 5 - Gratification: Orchestrating Pre-Launch Harmony:**

Clear articulation of pre-launch vision with the throat chakra's clarity.

Building community resonance through transparent communication.

Cultivating a culture of appreciation and anticipating/ mitigating challenges.

➢ **Third Eye Chakra - Day 6 - Glow: Illuminating Global Collaboration:**

Utilization of professional insight and a positive mindset for global collaboration.

Transcendental vision for holistic collaboration and embracing virtual communication tools.

Fostering cross-cultural sensitivity and illuminating the path of global unity.

➢ **Crown Chakra - Day 7 - Greatness: Ascending to Market Leadership:**

Channeling professional wisdom for strategic market positioning.

Aligning with a transcendental purpose beyond immediate success.

Integration of innovative features, holistic marketing campaigns, and a sustainable long-term vision.

Note:

'Attainments' and 'Applying the Dynamic 7G Transcendental Framework' were deliberately omitted, as they are encompassed within the section labeled 'Takeaways.'

"In the shadows of ambiguity, misinformation thrives, a silent saboteur of clarity and unity. Yet, with courage and transparency, we bring every truth into the light, disarming the potency of deception. As stewards of transformation, let our commitment to authenticity be the beacon that dispels the darkness and paves the way for enlightened leadership."

Episode #12:

Nature's Crucible: Cognos's Battle Against the Crisis Storm

The day had begun like any other at Cognos. The office buzzed with activity, a hive of employees dedicated to their roles, the excitement of the upcoming gaming platform launch hanging in the air like a promise of adventure. Routine meetings, coffee runs, and the constant hum of keyboards created a comforting cadence to the day.

But then, like a subtle breeze rustling through parched leaves, it began – a mere blog post, hidden in the recesses of the internet, ignited a smoldering fire. A cluster of influential bloggers, propelled by unclear motives, crafted an article hinting that the highly awaited platform launch of Cognos might be in jeopardy. Their assertions painted a grim picture, suggesting the company was teetering on the edge of financial depletion, casting shadows over the grand gaming dream.

As the morning sun inched higher in the sky, this spark of misinformation caught a gust of attention. Within hours, it was no longer a flicker but a full-blown blaze. While not all news channels had picked up the story, a few had, their sensationalist headlines fanning the flames.

By mid-morning, the situation at Cognos had escalated into a full-blown crisis, the kind that sent shockwaves not only through the company but across the entire gaming industry. It was a crisis that threatened to devour the company's reputation, along with the hopes and dreams of millions of gamers who had eagerly awaited the platform launch.

At the heart of this crisis was a kernel of truth, one that the bloggers and rumormongers had seized upon with avaricious glee. It was true that Cognos had faced financial challenges in the lead-up to the launch. Securing the necessary funds for a project of this magnitude had proven to be a herculean task, even for a company as ambitious as Cognos.

To bridge the financial gap, the company had reached out to sponsors, gaming industry partners willing to invest in the venture. These sponsors and the Virtual Gaming Federation weren't mere opportunists looking to exploit a struggling enterprise. They had recognized the potential in Cognos's vision and had genuinely stepped in to support what they believed was a promising and innovative gaming platform.

However, In the treacherous landscape of the internet, where sensationalism often held more sway than facts, this financial collaboration had been twisted into a narrative of impending catastrophe.

In the internet's volatile realm, sensationalism rules, distorting the financial collaboration into a looming disaster.

Bloggers portrayed Cognos as a sinking ship, foretelling its demise before it even began, feeding followers a misleading narrative. They speculated wildly about the company's financial health, conjuring doomsday scenarios that had no basis. With each passing hour, these narratives grew more feverish, feeding on the uncertainty that now clouded the company's future. Social media erupted with hashtags and discussions, and the mainstream media, always hungry for a juicy story, had begun to pick up on the frenzy.

In the relentless storm of attention-grabbing headlines, ominous forecasts swept through media channels. "Is Cognos Teetering on the Edge of Collapse?" blared one headline, while another screamed, "Financial Turmoil Threatens to Unravel Gaming Company's Much-Awaited Launch." This whirlwind of speculation not only cast a shadow on the company's image but also put at risk the faith of sponsors, partners, and the entire gaming community.

In a twist of events, another influential blogger heightened the stakes, leveling accusations against Cognos for allegedly partaking in practices detrimental to the environment. The blogger pointedly highlighted the environmental impact stemming from the constant demand for processing power and cooling systems, citing the potential creation of a substantial carbon footprint. This accusation acted as a catalyst, injecting more intensity into the burgeoning crisis, elevating apprehensions and significantly heightening the importance of Cognos' standing in terms of reputation and environmental accountability.

"The situation had escalated into a perfect storm, blending misinformation with genuine concern. The once thrilling countdown to our platform launch now resembled a ticking time bomb. The very industry we aimed to revolutionize was eyeing us skeptically, unsure if our promises would materialize or crumble into dust. Unfortunately, this will impact our relationships too," Vishwa admitted, feeling beads of sweat forming on his brow.

Losing advertisers' support could spell doom for Cognos. The financial strain from potential refunds alone might cripple the company, not to mention the irreparable damage to the hard-earned reputation.

As if that wasn't enough, the Gaming Commission, known for its strict adherence to transparency, had caught wind of the crisis rumours. Vishwa received a call from the Commission's formidable leader, emphasizing the critical nature of the situation. The warning was stark: "If the information continues in the media, it will harm the Commission's credibility, regardless of its truth. "

Vishwa hung up the phone, his knuckles white from the tension. The weight of the impending disaster bore down on him like a mountain threatening to collapse. It wasn't just the future of

Cognos at stake; it was the livelihoods of employees, the dreams of millions of gamers, and the very essence of the gaming industry's integrity.

Vishwa called for a Board Meeting and asked Ramji to join to discuss the way forward.

The boardroom at Cognos was alive with tension, everyone aware of the gravity of the crisis. Vishwa looked around the table, contemplating the suggestions presented by the heads of various departments. The tension was palpable as they grappled with the severity of the situation.

Mathur, the Marketing & Communications Manager, pitched a daring proposal for an epic advertising blitz to combat the allegations. His idea struck a chord with some members, offering a bold and attention-grabbing response—a direct confrontation to seize control of the narrative. Heads around the table nodded in agreement, recognizing the potential impact of such an assertive approach.

However, the head of legal was concerned about the time and potential legal implications. "Legal action takes time," they reiterated, emphasizing the need to protect the company's reputation without causing further escalation.

Ramji listened attentively to the proposals, nodding thoughtfully as each idea was presented. His tranquil presence amid the charged atmosphere provided a sense of calm.

Vishwa, inspired by Ramji's thoughtful demeanor, invoked the Socratic method, encouraging a deeper exploration of the proposed alternatives.

"Let's delve into the implications of each approach," Vishwa suggested, looking around the table. "What might be the unintended consequences of launching a massive advertising blitz?"

Mathur, spoke first, his tone reflective. "While it might grab attention and counter the false allegations, I think, it could inadvertently amplify the very misinformation we seek to counter."

The head of legal chimed in, emphasizing the potential legal ramifications. "We must consider the legal hurdles and the time it would take to initiate such a campaign. It might not yield immediate results and could lead to prolonged legal battles."

As the discussions progressed, the team contemplated the implications of each proposed strategy. The boardroom became a forum for thoughtful deliberation, with each member encouraged to critically examine the proposed courses of action.

Ramji interjected with a question that catalyzed the discussion further. "What if our responses inadvertently validate the misinformation? How can we ensure that our actions don't become the focal point of the crisis?"

This probing question led the team to ponder the risks of each approach. They discussed how an aggressive response could potentially backfire, and the legal and reputational risks associated with it.

As the deliberations continued, a consensus emerged that while a bold advertising campaign might seem compelling, its potential to exacerbate the issue outweighed its immediate impact. The legal complications and the risk of unintentionally drawing more attention to the crisis seemed too significant to ignore.

Ramji reclined in his chair, wearing a contemplative expression. "Let's refrain from adding fuel to the fire. Instead, our approach will be strategic and controlled. We'll directly and transparently address the false information, but without turning it into a headline story. Think of our responses as precise water drops on a fiery front, not a deluge that engulfs everything. The situation's impact could have been far worse if we hadn't undertaken pre-launch activities, guided by the 'Gratification' principle of the framework, propelled by the Throat Chakra."

The room seemed to breathe a collective sigh of relief. Ramji's approach offered a path forward that was both aggressive while being mindful of the nuances of their crisis. It was a plan inspired by nature's wisdom, where sometimes, less is more, and where a precisely calibrated attack, not chaos, would win the day.

However, many remained uncertain about its potential success. So, Vishwa took the initiative to break the ice, asking, "Can you take charge of the control room with just one week to go for the launch", he asked Ramji

Ramji leaned forward, his gaze unwavering, and his voice resonating with the wisdom gained through years of navigating crises. "Yes, I will," he affirmed, "I view it as my sacred duty to ensure the success of the launch. During this formidable onslaught of misinformation, I propose a strategy inspired by the tactics used in fighting forest fires. These principles, drawn from the wisdom of nature, will serve as my compass in this challenging time."

Ramji's entrance into the Control Room for Communication marked the beginning of a bold departure from conventional crisis management practices. The entire team at Cognos was acutely aware that Ramji's approach was a stark contrast to the modern strategies employed in media crises. It was as if they were embarking on an uncharted journey, guided not by the latest trends in public relations but by ancient principles rooted in nature.

Ramji proposed replacing urgency with careful consideration, reacting swiftly only when absolutely necessary. This change in pace was palpable, and it left many team members uneasy.

This approach seemed counterintuitive to some, especially in an era where viral content and sensationalism ruled the day. But Ramji's trust in ancient principles, in the wisdom of nature, was unwavering. He believed that by not engaging in a head-on battle with misinformation, they could avoid inadvertently fueling it.

The modern playbook for managing a media crisis often involved a barrage of press releases, aggressive interviews, and a constant stream of social media updates. It was a high-stakes game of offense, where the goal was to flood the information space with their narrative. But Ramji was proposing the opposite—a defensive strategy where they controlled the narrative not by amplifying it but by carefully containing and countering it.

The team now saw the merit in this approach, understanding that controlled responses could be more effective in containing the crisis without inadvertently fueling it.

Vishwa, acknowledging the decision, turned to Ramji. "Your analogy and guidance have helped us navigate this crisis. Your approach, inspired by nature's wisdom, resonates with our situation. Let's proceed with this controlled response strategy."

The room exuded a newfound sense of determination, the team ready to implement a strategy inspired by the wisdom of nature—a strategy that aimed not for immediate extinguishing but for the calculated containment and controlled decay of the falsehoods.

Ramji, Vishwa, and a formidable coalition comprising the legal, marketing, operations, and communication teams braced themselves for the imminent showdown. Ramji's counsel to the department heads was clear: refrain from direct intervention, but rather provide support to the team initiatives while adhering to the principles of the 7G approach and closely observing the team's learnings and actions.

Takeaways

- **Introduction of Nature-Inspired Strategy:** *Introduction of crisis management strategy inspired by the wisdom found in nature.*

  Significance of careful consideration and a controlled response during crisis situations.

- **Avoiding Sensationalism:** *Team discouraged from engaging in a direct confrontation with misinformation.*

  Team advised against inadvertently fueling the crisis by avoiding aggressive and sensational responses.

- **Precision in Communication:** *Precise and strategic responses to address false information directly.*

  Team to adopt a strategy resembling "precise water drops on a fiery front" rather than an overwhelming deluge.

- **Ancient Principles in Crisis Management:** *Departure from modern crisis management practices in favor of principles rooted in nature.*

- **Controlled Decay of Falsehoods:** *Strategy aiming for the calculated containment and controlled decay of misinformation.*

  Defensive approach to control the narrative rather than flooding the information space.

Attainments

- **Shift in Crisis Management Paradigm:** *Successfully induced a shift from conventional crisis management practices to an approach inspired by ancient principles.*

- ➤ **Controlled Response Strategy:** *Introduced and gained acceptance for a controlled response strategy aimed at containing and countering misinformation without fueling it.*

- ➤ **Team Alignment:** *Successfully aligned the team with the unconventional crisis management approach, fostering a sense of determination.*

- ➤ **Risk Mitigation:** *Contributed to mitigating risks associated with aggressive crisis management, including legal implications and unintentional escalation.*

- ➤ **Leadership in Crisis:** *Demonstrated effective leadership in a crisis by providing a clear and thoughtful strategy, instilling confidence in the team.*

- ➤ **Wisdom Application:** *Applied wisdom gained through years of experience to guide the team in navigating a complex crisis situation.*

- ➤ **Preparation for Battle:** *Prepared the team for the impending battle by introducing a strategy that prioritized precision, control, and containment.*

Applying the Dynamic 7G Transcendental Framework

Growth:

Fostered growth by introducing a unique crisis management approach that challenged conventional strategies.

Guidance:

Provided guidance by offering a method inspired by nature's wisdom for navigating the crisis.

Led the team to carefully consider the implications of proposed strategies and guided them to a controlled response.

Grit:

Displayed grit by proposing an unconventional strategy in the face of a severe crisis.

Encouraged the team to withstand the pressure of aggressive crisis management practices.

Gallantry:

Demonstrated gallantry by suggesting a path that goes against the current trends in crisis management.

Stood firm in advocating for a defensive strategy despite potential skepticism.

Gratitude:

Acknowledged the wisdom of nature and ancient principles as valuable sources of guidance.

Expressed gratitude for the team's willingness to embrace an unconventional crisis management approach.

Glow:

Radiated a calm and confident glow, providing reassurance to the team amid the crisis.

Created a positive atmosphere by introducing a strategy that offered a sense of control and stability.

Greatness:

Embarked on a journey guided by greatness, prioritizing a strategy focused on long-term containment rather than immediate extinguishing.

Demonstrated the greatness of strategic thinking by proposing a nuanced and thoughtful approach.

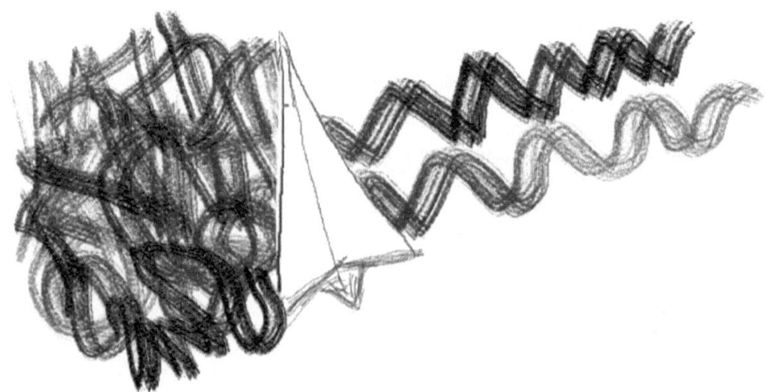

"Amid misinformation, we sculpt narratives, strategically controlling the spread, altering the information 'weather' to guide the course of truth through transparency and powerful communication"

Episode #13:

Compassion in Action: Transforming Challenges into Triumphs

In the heart of a forest, amidst the fierce dance of wildfire flames, Ramji's authoritative voice reverberated, reminiscent of a general leading his troops.

"Today marks Ground Zero of our battle—a pivotal moment amidst the inferno, mirroring the profound lesson embedded in our fight against the digital wildfire of misinformation. Just as the triad of fuel, weather, and natural barriers dictates the path of a wildfire, our strategy to combat misinformation hinges on manipulating these analogous factors.

In the realm of misinformation, fuel embodies the propagation of false narratives and deceptive information, akin to the sustenance a wildfire requires. Instead of extinguishing every misinformation spark immediately, our approach strategically tackles and curtails its spread, akin to controlling the fuel feeding a fire. Weather, influencing a fire's behavior, mirrors the dynamics of information dissemination. By altering the 'weather' of information through transparency, fact-checking, and strategic communication, we seek to influence the direction and intensity of false narratives.

Our preventive measures against misinformation align with natural barriers or topography — obstacles hindering the wildfire-like spread. Establishing these barriers involves strategically engaging key influencers and channels, much like creating firebreaks to contain a blaze. Furthermore, just as wildfires sometimes yield benefits to natural ecosystems, certain instances of misinformation, even if misleading, might inadvertently lead to positive outcomes.

As we navigate this digital wilderness, let us harness the wisdom of nature's wildfire behavior. Instead of hastily extinguishing every spark of misinformation, let us strategically control its spread until it naturally fades away. Let us be the stewards of truth in this digital age, recognizing the delicate balance between fighting falsehoods and allowing the natural course of information to unfold, much like letting a wildfire provide benefits such as improved wildlife habitat or fuel reduction."

With a surgical precision inspired by Ramji's insights, the team absorbed his wisdom, preparing themselves for the imminent battle.

Emphasizing the importance of a strategic pause, Ramji declared, "We embark on a journey akin to explorers charting uncharted territories. Our mission is to dissect this web of misinformation plaguing our digital realm. We're the seekers of truth in this labyrinth of falsehoods."

Their quest wasn't about immediate action but about understanding the landscape, identifying misinformation hotspots, and laying the groundwork for the days to come. The team absorbed Ramji's wisdom like a sponge, readying themselves for the strategic journey ahead.

With just seven days remaining until the highly anticipated launch, all of Cognos' teams were in high gear, leaving no stone unturned in their preparations. Every minute detail was meticulously attended to.

Recognizing the social media crisis as a critical obstacle, Ramji, alongside the legal, marketing, operations, and communication teams, took a hands-on approach, implementing the 7G Transcendental Framework in real-time, which Ramji had already introduced.

Ramji began by delving into the core principle of Growth, linking it to the root chakra—an emblem of stability, security, and a firm foundation. "Just as the root chakra grounds our energy, Growth acts as the cornerstone 'G' in our 7G Transcendental Framework, laying the groundwork for our journey into the digital realm," he elaborated.

The team soon engaged in exploratory discussions and analytical exercises, akin to tending to the roots of a mighty tree. They delved deep into the complexities of the digital realm, seeking to understand its intricacies while remaining firmly grounded in their purpose.

Ramji orchestrated a reflective activity designed to solidify the team's understanding of Growth and its implications for their mission. Gathering the team in a circle, he distributed sheets of paper and asked each member to write down their personal interpretations of growth in the context of the current situation.

One member highlighted the profound impact of algorithms within social media platforms, shaping the content users see based on their browsing history, preferences, and engagement patterns. They emphasized how these algorithms often prioritize engagement metrics like likes, shares, and comments, incentivizing the spread of sensationalist or emotionally charged content, regardless of its accuracy.

Another team member expanded on this insight, emphasizing how algorithms create echo chambers and filter bubbles, reinforcing users' existing beliefs and preferences while limiting exposure to diverse viewpoints. They noted how this phenomenon can exacerbate the spread of misinformation, as users are more likely to encounter and engage with content that aligns with their preconceived notions, regardless of its veracity.

As the discussion unfolded, a chorus of insights echoed through the room as more team members chimed in, each sharing their unique observations. Some illuminated the role of artificial intelligence in fine-tuning content recommendations, while others delved into the ethical implications of algorithmic bias and manipulation. Together, they painted a vibrant and intricate tableau of the digital landscape, where misinformation thrives, fueled by the algorithms that wield power over our digital interactions.

This exchange of ideas became the catalyst for a profound shift within the team. By diving deeper into these insights, they cultivated a heightened awareness of the multifaceted challenges lying ahead in the battle against misinformation. The realization dawned that countering false narratives required not just understanding but a strategic navigation of the complex algorithms dictating reach and impact. Armed with strategies to counteract biases and disrupt echo chambers, the team was poised for their purpose-driven journey into the digital wilderness.

Under the leadership of Ramji, the team swiftly transitioned into action mode. Placing a premium on authenticity and trust, they harnessed their collective understanding of the impact of algorithms within social media platforms. Their content creation efforts became a beacon of authenticity and trust, countering the algorithmic pull towards sensationalism with messages that were accurate, transparent, and emotionally resonant.

Recognizing the algorithms as the gatekeepers of content visibility, the team strategically tailored their messages to harmonize with these digital gatekeepers. By optimizing content for algorithms, they ensured wider dissemination without compromising accuracy or reliability. Ethical considerations were woven into their content creation process, guarding against manipulative tactics that could inadvertently contribute to misinformation.

Embracing the dynamic pulse of the digital realm, the team transformed into vigilant custodians of content. Their daily routine evolved into a meticulous dance of continuous content monitoring, metric analysis, and a sharp focus on the ever-changing algorithms governing the digital landscape. This adaptive stance empowered them to tweak strategies on the fly, ensuring agility and effectiveness in navigating the intricate web of deception.

Aware that dismantling this complex web couldn't happen overnight, everyone embraced the understanding that persistent communication on social media was key. Each day became a building block, contributing to the gradual unraveling of the falsehood tapestry.

Ramji, recognizing the team's swift comprehension and adaptability in this critical juncture, showered praise. The team exuded a tangible sense of purpose and determination, laying the groundwork for the upcoming chapter in their unyielding quest for truth in the vast digital wilderness.

Ramji plunged into the essence of the second principle: Guidance. He likened it to the Sacral Chakra, a hub of creativity and emotional equilibrium. Much like how the Sacral Chakra channels guidance, urging individuals to harness their creative instincts and emotional wisdom, Guidance illuminated the path for the team's journey of resilience and innovation

The team immersed themselves in discussions and exercises aimed at honing their creative problem-solving skills and emotional intelligence. Ramji led them through a series of guided meditations and reflective exercises, encouraging them to tap into their inner reservoirs of creativity and empathy.

As the team delved deeper into the concept of Guidance, they explored strategies for fostering emotional intelligence and empathy in their approach to combating misinformation. They discussed the importance of understanding the motivations and emotions driving the spread of false narratives, as well as the power of empathy in effectively communicating the truth.

Ramji encouraged the team to embrace their creative instincts and think outside the box when developing strategies to counter misinformation. They brainstormed innovative approaches to engage with audiences, leveraging storytelling, visual media, and other creative mediums to effectively communicate accurate information.

The team's discussions were infused with a sense of openness and exploration, as they embraced the creative potential of the Sacral Chakra. They recognized that by tapping into their emotional intelligence and creativity, they could develop more impactful and empathetic approaches to combating misinformation, setting the stage for their journey into the digital wilderness with renewed inspiration and purpose.

Ramji orchestrated a creative activity designed to deepen the team's understanding of Guidance and its practical implications for their mission. Gathering the team in a circle, he distributed blank canvases and an assortment of art supplies, inviting each member to express their interpretations of Guidance through art.

With paintbrushes in hand and minds open to inspiration, the team embarked on a journey of creative exploration. Some chose to depict scenes of guidance and mentorship, capturing the essence of emotional support and encouragement. Others expressed the concept of guidance through abstract forms and colors, tapping into their inner creativity to convey the flow of guidance in visual form.

As the room filled with the sound of brushes on canvas and the vibrant hues of creativity, the team embraced the opportunity to channel their emotions and insights into tangible expressions of Guidance. Through their artwork, they explored the interconnectedness of creativity, emotional intelligence, and guidance, gaining a deeper appreciation for the role these elements play.

As the final brushstrokes were made and the last colors blended, the team gathered to share their creations and reflect on the experience. Each artwork served as a unique reflection of the team member's understanding of Guidance, offering new perspectives and insights into the power of creativity and emotional intelligence in their work.

Immersing themselves in this creative activity not only tightened the team's bonds and kindled a sense of camaraderie but also unearthed profound insights into the practical applications of Guidance.

Inspired by their fresh insights, Ramji led the team on a transformative quest to create blog posts infused with emotional intelligence. These weren't mere data dumps; they became intricate tapestries of storytelling, weaving together facts, emotions, and audience concerns. Leveraging creative narratives and captivating visuals, they skillfully conveyed the company's stance. Through this artful communication, they not only debunked misconceptions but also cultivated a garden of trust and empathy among stakeholders.

As the day concluded, the team didn't just leave, they departed inspired and energized. Armed with their harnessed creativity and emotional intelligence, they stood ready to face the impending challenges with an unshakeable confidence and a resolute purpose.

With only 6 day left, Ramji led the team on a journey into the principle of Grit, drawing parallels with the Solar Plexus Chakra, which represents the seat of personal power and determination. Just as the Solar Plexus Chakra empowers individuals to overcome obstacles and persevere in the face of challenges, Grit served as the driving force behind the team's resilience and determination.

The team engaged in discussions and exercises focused on cultivating grit and resilience in their approach to tackling misinformation. Ramji shared inspiring stories of individuals who had demonstrated extraordinary grit in the face of adversity, encouraging the team to draw inspiration from their examples.

As the team delved deeper into the concept of Grit, they explored strategies for building resilience and perseverance in the face of challenges. They discussed the importance of maintaining a positive mindset and staying focused on their goals, even in the face of setbacks and obstacles.

Ramji challenged the team to reflect on their own experiences of overcoming adversity and tapping into their inner reservoirs of grit and determination. Through guided exercises and self-reflection, team members identified their strengths and areas for growth, harnessing the power of grit to propel them forward in their mission.

The team's discussions were infused with a sense of determination and resolve, as they embraced the power of the Solar Plexus Chakra to fuel their efforts. They recognized that by cultivating grit and resilience, they could overcome any obstacle in their path and emerge stronger and more resilient than ever before.

Ramji orchestrated a reflective activity designed to deepen the team's understanding of Grit and its practical implications for their mission. Gathering the team in a circle, he invited each member to share a personal story of overcoming adversity and tapping into their inner grit.

With hearts open and spirits fortified, team members shared stories of triumph and resilience, inspiring and uplifting one another with tales of perseverance and determination. Through this shared experience, the team strengthened their bonds and reaffirmed their commitment to tackling misinformation with unwavering resolve.

By engaging in this reflective activity, the team not only deepened their understanding of Grit but also strengthened their sense of camaraderie and mutual support. They felt empowered and emboldened, ready to face whatever challenges lay ahead with courage and determination.

Building on the journey inspired by Ramji's challenge, team members wove their personal triumphs over adversity into the fabric of the blog posts. These narratives transformed setbacks into stories of resilience and determination, humanizing the team and reinforcing the profound message that challenges can be surmounted with unwavering grit.

Guided by Ramji's unparalleled understanding of Grit, the team evolved into advocates, mobilizing employees to champion the cause. Through personal social media accounts, their authentic voices resonated, countering the impact of misinformation. The call was clear: share personal stories aligning with the company's narrative of resilience.

Harnessing the tightly-knit camaraderie within the team, they forged a unified front across social media platforms. Team members shared, retweeted, and engaged with each other's posts, creating a collective online presence that echoed the resounding message of resilience and determination. Together, they became a force against misinformation.

Internally, communication channels were fortified, ensuring all the teams across the company remained well-informed about ongoing efforts. Regular updates on misinformation mitigation strategies, coupled with accounts of successes and challenges, fostered a shared understanding and ignited a collective sense of purpose. In this shared journey, each team member became a vital part of the mission.

Individual efforts were not only recognized but celebrated. Instances where team members actively contributed to misinformation mitigation were highlighted, becoming beacons of inspiration. This appreciation not only boosted morale but also underscored the pivotal role each team member played in the collective fight against this crisis.

The team thrived on open communication and a culture of constructive feedback. This environment ensured continuous adaptation and evolution in their mission. Each suggestion, insight, and lesson learned became a building block, shaping a more resilient and effective strategy.

As the journey unfolded, Ramji stood at the helm, guiding the team with wisdom and encouragement. In acknowledging the team's profound understanding and rapid adaptation to the mission, Ramji expressed his heartfelt appreciation. The collective effort, fueled by personal narratives, camaraderie, and adaptive strategies, epitomized the team's commitment to truth and authenticity.

Ramji led the team on a journey into the principle of Gallantry, drawing parallels with the Heart Chakra, which represents compassion and ethical balance. Just as the Heart Chakra guides individuals on a path of ethical conduct, Gallantry served as the guiding light for the team's actions, fostering compassion and integrity in their mission.

The team delved into discussions and exercises focused on embodying gallantry in their approach to tackling misinformation. Ramji shared examples of individuals who had demonstrated exceptional compassion and integrity in their work, inspiring the team to uphold similar values in their efforts.

The team's discussions were infused with a sense of compassion and empathy, as they sought to embody the principles of the Heart Chakra in their work. They recognized that by acting with integrity and compassion, they could not only combat misinformation but also foster a more harmonious and sustainable digital ecosystem.

Ramji orchestrated a reflective activity designed to deepen the team's understanding of Gallantry and its practical implications for their mission. Gathering the team in a circle, he invited each member to share a personal story of a time when they had demonstrated compassion and integrity in their work.

With hearts open and minds focused, team members shared stories of moments when they had acted with courage and compassion, inspiring and uplifting one another with their shared experiences. Through this collective reflection, the team strengthened their commitment to upholding ethical conduct and compassion.

By engaging in this reflective activity, the team not only deepened their understanding of Gallantry but also reaffirmed their dedication to making a positive impact on the world through their actions. They felt empowered and inspired, ready to continue their journey with compassion and integrity as their guiding principles.

Encouraged by Ramji's acknowledgment, the team found renewed vigor in their mission. The ripple effects of their compassionate initiatives were palpable within and beyond the organization.

To expand their impact, the team crafted a multimedia series featuring personal stories of resilience and compassion. These narratives transcended the digital realm, resonating with a global audience. The team's online presence transformed into a beacon of hope and authenticity, countering the waves of misinformation with genuine human experiences.

The empathy workshops, now an integral part of the team's culture, evolved into interactive sessions where members openly shared their empathetic breakthroughs. This continuous learning loop not only fortified the team's internal bonds but also cultivated a profound understanding of the diverse perspectives they aimed to reach.

In tandem, the team's volunteer initiatives gained momentum, evolving into a sustainable community outreach program. They collaborated with local organizations, creating a network that fortified the resilience of communities against the onslaught of misinformation. The team became not just defenders of truth but active contributors to the well-being of society.

Amidst these endeavors, the commitment to self-reflection became a powerful catalyst for innovation. The team initiated a knowledge-sharing platform, where insights gained from their journey were disseminated. This not only empowered the team but also engaged a wider community in the collective fight against misinformation.

Ramji, witnessing the team's evolution, acknowledged their transformative impact. He emphasized that their journey was not just a campaign against misinformation; it was a movement to redefine how authenticity and integrity could prevail in the digital landscape. The team, fueled by this recognition, stood united and resolute, ready to face the evolving challenges with compassion, integrity, and a shared commitment to truth.

Undeterred and riding the wave of momentum from the live implementation of the 7G framework, the team surged ahead with unwavering determination. Far from simply maintaining the status quo, they underwent a metamorphosis, transforming each undertaking into a powerful stepping stone for a more influential and dynamic journey. The collective spirit of the team reached new heights, driving them into the next phase of their mission with a shared resolve reverberating through every action and initiative.

Armed with a deep understanding of the introduced 7Gs in action, the team continued their proactive efforts for days to come. Ramji, displaying his leadership prowess, engaged with stakeholders to identify and eliminate any potential bottlenecks for the upcoming Virtual Gaming Platform launch. He conducted thorough checks across compliance, legal, and various business domains, ensuring that every aspect was meticulously on track for the impending launch. The team's commitment to excellence was palpable, setting the stage for a groundbreaking and seamless entry into the virtual gaming arena.

Vishwa meticulously oversaw the comprehensive check-list, leaving nothing to chance and ensuring absolute control over every crucial element. The anticipation soared, promising enthusiasts an unforgettable experience on the brink of unfolding.

With 2 days left for launch, Ramji guided the team through the principle of Gratification, drawing parallels with the Throat Chakra, which represents communication and expression. Just as the Throat Chakra encourages individuals to express their achievements and joys, Gratification urged the team to find fulfillment not only in their actions but also in articulating the beauty of their journey.

The team engaged in activities and discussions centered around celebrating their progress and finding joy in their collective journey. Ramji encouraged team members to reflect on their achievements and share their experiences with one another, fostering a sense of camaraderie and appreciation for their hard work.

As the team reflected on their accomplishments, they found themselves filled with a sense of gratification and pride. They shared stories of challenges overcome, milestones achieved, and lessons learned, celebrating each other's successes and supporting one another through setbacks during this social media crisis.

Ramji challenged the team to vocalize their gratification, encouraging them to express their appreciation for one another and acknowledge the contributions of their colleagues. Through open and honest communication, the team deepened their connections and strengthened their bonds, united by a shared sense of purpose and achievement.

Ramji orchestrated a celebratory activity designed to honor the team's achievements and express their gratitude to one another. Gathering in a circle, he invited each member to share a moment of gratification from their journey so far, whether it be a personal milestone, a team success, or a lesson learned.

With hearts full and voices lifted, team members took turns expressing their gratitude and appreciation for one another, celebrating the collective effort that had brought them to this point. Through laughter, tears, and heartfelt words, they found fulfillment not only in their actions but also in the connections they had forged along the way in handling this crisis.

The team wove a tapestry of captivating blog posts, illuminating their transformative journey with a spotlight on transparency and authentic communication. Extending a warm invitation, they beckoned the audience to join their odyssey, fostering inclusivity and openness. Through the vivid portrayal of their mission's beauty and an unwavering commitment to address concerns head-on, the team not only set out to counter misinformation but also endeavored to construct a foundation of trust and mutual understanding among their stakeholders.

In the face of environmental accusations, Ramji, guided by the Throat Chakra's essence of authentic communication, orchestrated a harmonious response for Cognos. Focusing on the Gratification principle, he instilled a sense of purpose and pride within the team as they worked towards mitigating the alleged environmental impact.

Collaborating closely with Vishwa and department heads, Ramji meticulously developed ESG and Corporate Governance strategies at Cognos, all transparent and in line with the essence of the Throat Chakra. With Ramji at the helm, Cognos wholeheartedly embraced openness, directly addressing concerns and shedding light on ongoing and future initiatives to reduce the company's carbon footprint. It wasn't just about strategy; it was a firm commitment to nurturing a well-informed and supportive user community. Amidst challenges, Ramji not only shielded Cognos' reputation but also cemented deeper, more resilient connections with stakeholders, paving the way for sustained business triumph.

Ramji's emphasis on Gratification played a crucial role in the team's response. By fostering a shared sense of accomplishment and purpose through environmental initiatives, he turned the crisis into an opportunity for Cognos to showcase its commitment to sustainable and responsible business practices. This alignment with the Throat Chakra and the Gratification principle not only addressed the immediate concerns but also set the stage for long-term positive engagement with the gaming community.

As has been the tradition for the past few days, Ramji, with genuine appreciation, applauded the collective efforts and triumphant achievements of the team.

Ramji next delved into the principle of Glow, drawing parallels with the Third Eye Chakra, which symbolizes insight, intuition, and a positive mindset that illuminates the path ahead. Just as the Third Eye Chakra fosters collaboration and interconnectedness, Glow urged the team to shine collectively and harness their intuition to navigate the challenges ahead.

The team engaged in activities and discussions focused on fostering insight, intuition, and collaboration. Ramji encouraged team members to trust their instincts and share their unique perspectives, recognizing that their collective wisdom would illuminate the path forward.

As the team explored the concept of Glow, they found themselves inspired by the power of collaboration and the insights that emerged from their collective efforts. They embraced the interconnectedness of their diverse backgrounds and experiences, recognizing that together, they were greater than the sum of their parts, implementing the Diversity, Equity, and Inclusion (DEI) policies.

Ramji facilitated discussions on intuition and encouraged team members to tap into their inner wisdom as they navigated complex challenges. Through mindfulness exercises and guided meditation, he helped the team cultivate a positive mindset and develop a deeper understanding of their individual and collective strengths.

As the day progressed, the team's insights deepened, and they found themselves approaching their work with newfound clarity and purpose. They embraced the interconnectedness of their efforts, recognizing that by working together, they could overcome any obstacle and achieve their shared goals.

Ramji orchestrated a reflective activity designed to solidify the team's understanding of Glow and its implications for their work. Gathering in a circle, he invited each member to share a moment of insight or intuition that had guided them on their journey so far.

Through open and honest dialogue, the team shared their experiences and perspectives, deepening their connections and reaffirming their commitment to collaboration and collective growth. By embracing the principles of Glow, they illuminated the path forward and prepared themselves for the challenges and opportunities that lay ahead.

Ramji guided the team through the principle of Greatness, drawing parallels with the Crown Chakra, the highest point of spiritual connection. Just as the Crown Chakra transcends individual success, Greatness urged the team to aspire for a legacy that would contribute to the collective greatness of their professional realm.

The team engaged in reflective exercises and discussions focused on their aspirations for greatness and their vision for the future. Ramji encouraged team members to connect with their higher purpose and consider how their actions could leave a lasting impact on their organization and industry.

As the team explored the concept of Greatness, they reflected on their individual and collective journeys, recognizing the potential they had to make a meaningful difference in the world. They shared stories of inspiration and discussed the values that drove them to strive for excellence in their work.

Ramji facilitated discussions on legacy and encouraged team members to envision the impact they wanted to have on future generations. Through guided visualization exercises, he helped the team connect with their innermost desires and aspirations, empowering them to take bold action in pursuit of their dreams.

The team's discussions grew more profound, and they found themselves inspired by the possibilities that lay ahead. They embraced the idea of contributing to the collective greatness of their professional realm, recognizing that their individual efforts had the power to shape the course of history.

As the day drew to a close, Ramji orchestrated a culminating activity designed to solidify the team's understanding of Greatness and its implications for their work. Gathering in a circle, he invited each member to share their vision for the future and commit to taking concrete steps toward achieving their goals.

Through heartfelt dialogue and shared commitment, the team reaffirmed their dedication to excellence and pledged to work together to create a legacy that would endure for generations to come. By embracing the principle of Greatness, they set themselves on a path toward a future defined by purpose, passion, and profound impact.

As the hands-on immersive learning and reflection drew to a close, the team found themselves on the brink of a profound realization. Guided by Ramji's wisdom and the principles of the 7G Transcendental Framework, they had embarked on a journey of self-discovery and collective growth, laying the groundwork for their mission to combat misinformation with purpose and determination.

Vishwa, along with department heads and teams, showered Ramji with heartfelt appreciation for guiding them through the social media crisis and implementing the 7G framework. Vishwa continued, acknowledging that Ramji's wisdom would remain with the team, serving as a beacon in navigating future challenges with calmness and composure. The learnings gained by all teams were immense and invaluable. Everyone rose to their feet, applauding Ramji's leadership.

As the sun slipped beneath the horizon, its fading light casting dramatic shadows, Ramji stood tall amidst the team. His aura radiated inspiration and wisdom, a guiding light in the dimming room. With genuine gratitude, he commended everyone for their unwavering dedication towards Continuous Learning and Relentless Improvement. Reflecting on their journey, he marveled at the profound transformations and the strong bonds forged in the crucible of shared experience

"Now, my dear friends," Ramji began, his voice resonating with warmth and conviction, "we stand at the threshold of greatness, poised to embark on the next chapter of our journey. But before we take that leap forward, let us take a moment to reflect on the lessons we have learned and the wisdom we have gained."

"In the days to come, we will face new challenges and obstacles," Ramji continued, his words imbued with a sense of quiet confidence. "But as long as we remain true to our values and committed to our mission, there is nothing that can stand in our way."

With renewed determination and a shared sense of purpose, the team prepared to embark on the next chapter of their journey, the one that will determine the fate of the Virtual Gaming Industry.

On the penultimate day, the tide of misinformation surrounding Cognos subsided. News reports on social media platforms, once rampant with sensationalism and clickbait, gradually faded away. The digital landscape, often preoccupied with fleeting trends and daily gossip, swiftly moved on from the incident. Those with a discerning understanding of the situation recognized it as a calculated manoeuvre, and the consensus was that no substantial damage had been inflicted. In this manner, the episode became a transient blip, overshadowed by the ever-shifting focus of online narratives.

The elation among all stakeholders of Cognos was palpable as the storm of misinformation finally lifted. Joy and relief reverberated through the corridors of the company, from the developers and business analysts to the marketing team and sponsors. The collective sigh of relief echoed the sentiment that the integrity of Cognos had been preserved.

As the dust settled, the Virtual Gaming Federation, recognizing the exceptional efforts and leadership demonstrated by Ramji in navigating the crisis, extended a prestigious invitation. Ramji was invited to be the guest of honour and inaugurate the highly anticipated gaming event. This invitation wasn't just a recognition of an individual; it was a testament to the triumph of resilience, strategic acumen, and a commitment to transparency.

Amidst the fervor surrounding Ramji's upcoming address, Cognos unveiled an innovative tool within their virtual platform, adding to the anticipation. The tool, named "EcoLens," is a virtual communication tool with 3D capabilities and taking the virtual gaming experience of the audience to the next level. It also showcased real-time data illustrating the environmental impact of gaming choices, fostering a new level of eco-consciousness among players. Its seamless integration into the platform signaled Cognos's commitment to sustainability, aligning with Ramji's ethos of leadership inspired by nature.

As the clock struck the much-anticipated moment, the audience held their breath in anticipation of Ramji's address. Suddenly, the EcoLens tool's interface subtly emerged on screens, captivating millions worldwide. It was a watershed moment, blending gaming excitement with environmental consciousness, showcasing Cognos's commitment to pioneering responsible gaming.

In the virtual auditorium, a global audience buzzed with excitement, eager to witness Ramji's groundbreaking address. The camera swept across a mosaic of faces, reflecting the diverse tapestry of the gaming community, united in their anticipation.

Takeaways

- **Strategic Approach to Misinformation:** *Combat misinformation strategically, controlling its spread until natural fading.*

  Inspired by the analogy of wildfires, manipulating fuel, weather, and barriers.

- **Understanding Growth in Digital Landscape:** *Growth as a foundational principle in the 7G Transcendental Framework.*

  Explore algorithms, echo chambers, and AI on social media platforms.

- **Harnessing Creativity and Emotional Intelligence:** *Embrace Guidance, linked to the Sacral Chakra.*

  Develope impactful approaches through creative expression and emotionally intelligent blog posts.

- **Cultivating Grit and Resilience:** *Grit principle, linked to the Solar Plexus Chakra.*

  Explored strategies for positivity, focus, and drawing inspiration from stories of grit.

- ➤ **Ethical Conduct and Compassion:** *Deepened understanding of Gallantry, linked to the Heart Chakra.*

  Balanced ambition with compassion, fostering a harmonious digital ecosystem.

- ➤ **Expressing Gratitude and Celebrating Achievements:** *Gratification principle, linked to the Throat Chakra.*

  Celebrated progress, vocalized gratitude, and articulated the beauty of the journey.

- ➤ **Insight, Intuition, and Collaboration:** *Glow principle, linked to the Third Eye Chakra.*

  Fostered insight, intuition, and collaboration through mindfulness and shared experiences.

- ➤ **Aspiring for Collective Greatness:** *Greatness principle, linked to the Crown Chakra.*

  Aspired for a legacy contributing to the collective greatness of their professional realm.

Attainments

- ➤ **Strategic Implementation of 7G Framework:** *Aligned each principle with the mission to combat misinformation.*

  Comprehensive understanding, adaptive content creation, and ethical considerations.

- ➤ **Adaptive Content Creation:** *Countered algorithmic biases, disrupted echo chambers.*

  Strategically tailored messages for wider dissemination without compromising accuracy.

- ➤ **Community Engagement and Outreach:** *Extended impact through multimedia series, volunteer initiatives, and knowledge-sharing platforms.*

Engaged with a wider audience, contributing to community resilience against misinformation.

➤ **Positive Environmental Response:** *Implemented transparent communication strategy aligned with the Throat Chakra.*

Showcased commitment to sustainability, turning crisis into an opportunity for positive engagement.

➤ **Building a Resilient Culture:** *Cultivated resilience through open communication, constructive feedback, and continuous adaptation.*

Recognized and celebrated individual efforts, contributing to a shared understanding.

➤ **Humanizing the Mission:** *Infused communication with empathy and creativity.*

Blog posts became narratives, dispelling rumors and building trust.

➤ **Global Impact:** *Efforts showcased globally through multimedia series and online presence.*

Countered misinformation waves with genuine human experiences, fostering inclusivity.

Applying the Dynamic 7G Transcendental Framework

Growth (Root Chakra):

Understanding algorithms, echo chambers, and AI.

Strategic engagement with influencers and channels for barriers against misinformation.

Guidance (Sacral Chakra):

Hone creative problem-solving skills and emotional intelligence.

Crafted emotionally intelligent blog posts and diversified content approaches.

Grit (Solar Plexus Chakra):

Building resilience and perseverance.

Mobilized employees, shared personal stories, and became advocates against misinformation.

Gallantry (Heart Chakra):

Fostering compassion and ethical balance.

Crafted transparent communication strategy, addressing environmental concerns.

Gratification (Throat Chakra):

Vocalizing achievements and joys.

Expressed gratitude, celebrated progress, and articulated the beauty of the journey.

Glow (Third Eye Chakra):

Fostering insight, intuition, and collaboration.

Trusted instincts, engaged in mindfulness exercises, and deepened connections.

Greatness (Crown Chakra):

Aspiring for a legacy contributing to collective greatness.

Reflected on individual and collective journeys, connecting with higher purpose.

"In the forge of ceaseless challenges and unwavering pressure, triumph adorns the odyssey, forged by resilience and communal vigor. Amidst tempests, steering with nature's wisdom turns adversity into victory—a collective testament to shared resilience, purpose, and the innate wisdom guiding through every storm."

Episode #14:

The Tide of Triumph: A Journey of Resilience and Collective Vigor

Amidst the fervor, leaders from the Virtual Gaming Federation, alongside Vishwa and the Cognos Marketing team head, unveiled the platform's visionary roadmap, enticing stakeholders with its transformative capabilities. A captivating demo followed, offering a tantalizing glimpse into the platform's immersive features.

With the atmosphere pulsating with excitement, Vishwa smoothly transitioned the spotlight to Ramji, igniting thunderous applause from the audience. "Let's warmly welcome Ramji," he proclaimed, paving the way for an enthralling voyage through Ramji's life journey and the unveiling of the Cognos Virtual Gaming Platform. And so, Ramji stepped onto the stage, poised to unveil a new era of gaming innovation.

Ramji took-off

"Ladies and gentlemen, gamers and enthusiasts, today, I have the distinct honor of standing before you not merely as the creator of the groundbreaking framework, "The 7G Transcendental Framework," but as a fervent disciple of the profound principles that nature, in its boundless wisdom, has generously bestowed upon us.

You know, I used to be that shy boy and my name was Paul. Paul always sat at the back of the class, always trying to blend into the walls rather than stand out. Just the idea of talking in front of my classmates would make me nervous. I'd find ways to avoid seminars and presentations, just so I wouldn't have to face the judgment I thought was coming my way.

My friends, they could be brutally honest sometimes, and they called me "boring Paul," like I couldn't keep anyone's attention. Those words hurt, but they also sparked something in me. Deep inside, I believed there was more to me than just being quiet. I had this urge to share my thoughts, to connect with people, to be interesting.

But changing wasn't easy. It was like a journey that started with a realization – I understood that real success isn't solely about stepping out of the comfort zone, but rather about how many lives were positively impacted by me. Stepping out of the comfort zone, however, enables this greater purpose. I needed to be brave enough to speak up, to build relationships, and to solve problems.

As the journey unfolded, a new chapter emerged when an organization beckoned, promising prosperity at first glance. Yet, delving deeper revealed concealed fissures lurking beneath the surface.

Communication was a mess, teams were isolated, and things were falling apart. It reminded me of the mistakes that led to Kodak's downfall.

Colleagues at odds, engaged in constant conflict instead of collaborating, prioritizing personal victories over the company's advancement. It created a toxic atmosphere, suffocating creativity and hindering progress. Internal politics reached its peak, overshadowing the collective goals.

And then, like a sad song, the organization started crumbling. It was hard to watch – a collective failure caused by misunderstandings and fights.

The impact was heartbreaking. People lost jobs, dreams were shattered, families suffered. It hit me hard – organizations have a responsibility not just to their profits, but to the people who rely on them and the society as a whole.

Aware of the necessary steps, there lingered a fear of speaking out. The apprehension of being judged or disliked kept me silent.

However, amidst the ruins, a profound shift occurred within. A stirring sense of duty took root, compelling action in the face of adversity. The passive observer transformed into an impassioned advocate for change.

In the whirlwind of corporate affairs, a haven was unearthed within the untouched tranquility of nature's embrace. Journeys into the forest became sanctuaries, offering solace in the quiet moments spent alone.

From the vast expanse of the forest ecosystem, the significance of interconnectedness was gleaned. Just as the trees communicated through their intricate root systems, organizations were urged to nurture open channels of communication and collaboration among their teams. It became evident that collective efforts yielded greater potency than individual endeavors.

The cycles of nature also held invaluable insights. Seasons changed, organisms adapted, and evolution was a constant. It dawned on me that organizations, too, needed to embrace change and evolve to thrive. This meant creating a culture of continuous learning, where growth was not merely a goal but a way of life.

I observed how nature operated in harmony, with each element playing a vital role in the greater ecosystem. I saw how diversity and inclusion were not just buzzwords, but the keys to a resilient and thriving environment. It made me realize the significance of building diverse teams, where different perspectives converged to create innovative e solutions.

Being the reserved one, the prospect of public speaking always sent shivers down my spine. Determined to conquer this fear, I delved into the realms of storytelling and public speaking. Books became my companions, and countless hours were spent in the library, absorbing every ounce of knowledge available. Along the way, I sought guidance from mentors who played a pivotal role in shaping my transformation.

I gained a unique perspective to help organizations from the time I spent in the forest. I went in as Paul but came back as Ramji. The failures I saw became lessons, and the pain turned into a way to understand others. Coaching wasn't about having all the answers; it was about helping others find their own way through challenges.

With the wisdom gained from my journey and an intense desire to catalyze change, the urge to explore new horizons became irresistible. Yet, lingering doubts and fears haunted my thoughts – what if the same fate awaited me as those organizations I sought to help?

The first organization that sought guidance presented a familiar tale, reminiscent of my past experiences. Internal conflicts, communication breakdowns, and a lack of alignment had steered them towards trouble. However, armed with acquired knowledge, the journey to untangle the web of miscommunication began. Witnessing the transformation unfold—from chaos to clarity, from discord to harmony—was undeniably gratifying.

As word spread about the successes, I was helping organizations achieve, more and more who sought my assistance. Each new challenge was a unique puzzle to solve, but the principles I had learned guided me like a compass. Together, we dismantled silos, bridged gaps in communication, and kindled a culture of shared purpose. It was about more than just profits; it was about restoring a sense of unity and shared vision.

There was an organization teetering on the edge of collapse, torn apart by internal power struggles. Guiding them towards realignment, the focus shifted from individual ambitions to collective growth. Witnessing egos dissolve and a genuine commitment to the organization's well-being emerge was truly heartening.

Another organization was grappling with a lack of creativity and innovation. By introducing nature-inspired learning principles, we ignited a spark of curiosity and exploration. Collaboration flourished, and the once-muted voices of their employees now resonated with brilliant ideas.

These stories of transformation weren't just about fixing surface-level problems; they were about igniting a profound cultural shift. As we all know, culture takes decades to be built and evolves gradually over time. Changing it for the better demand's patience and persistent effort. It wasn't always easy; there were moments of resistance and setbacks.

Nevertheless, the journey underscored the importance of resilience and unwavering belief in the process. I discovered that cultural transformation requires a guiding mentor and unwavering dedication from the entire team. Slowly but steadily, the impact of my work began to spread far and wide. Organizations that were once on the brink of collapse were now thriving, their people reinvigorated and united. Families were no longer torn apart by the fallout of organizational failures; they were flourishing together, thanks to the stability and growth their workplaces provided.

It wasn't just a job for me; it was a calling. Every organization I helped was a step towards fulfilling my commitment to prevent others from experiencing the pain I had witnessed. I understood the weight of my responsibility, and I embraced it wholeheartedly.

In the pursuit of empowering organizations and individuals, the 7G framework wasn't born from textbooks but from the boundless inspiration of nature. The intricate workings of the natural world became my muse, guiding me towards insights that could redefine success. The 7G framework was driven by a deep desire to usher in enduring success, blending the timeless principles of nature with the ever-evolving needs of the corporate world.

Ramji unveiled the 7G framework, a culmination of his personal journey and a tribute to the wisdom of nature. This framework distilled the essence of natural principles into actionable steps for professional development. Each element—Growth, Guidance, Grit, Gallantry, Gratification, Glow, and Greatness—reflected the intricate balance observed in nature. With its dynamic nature, the 7G Transcendental Framework adapts seamlessly to any situation at hand, offering a versatile tool for growth and success.

Growth was fundamental. I likened it to a seed's drive to become a tree, absorbing knowledge and nourishment from surroundings. Understanding the patterns of misinformation was crucial—much like studying the behavior of a forest fire—to tackle this crisis head-on.

Guidance, akin to mentorship in nature, was essential. I sought wisdom from communication and ethics experts. Learning from their strategies, I merged their insights with nature's resilience to navigate this crisis effectively.

Grit became our armor. We stood firm against the waves of misinformation, refusing to let falsehoods overshadow truth. It was about endurance, much like how trees weather storms without breaking.

Gallantry guided our actions. Upholding ethical conduct was paramount. Our efforts aligned with nature's principles of balance and truth, ensuring our battle against misinformation remained ethical.

Gratification fueled us. Celebrating each corrected fact, finding joy in the journey—similar to the bloom of a flower—kept morale high amidst this challenging task.

Glow fostered collaboration, echoing the harmony in ecosystems. Each team member contributed unique skills, working together effectively to counter misinformation.

Greatness was our aim. Beyond debunking, we aimed to educate and empower the community, leaving a legacy of informed thinking—much like contributing to the collective excellence of a field in nature.

Over the span of seven days, the team embarked on a mission resembling the journey through the seven chakras, navigating challenges akin to energy centers within the human body. Grounded in rooting out misinformation and guided by wisdom, resilience, ethics, celebration, collaboration, and legacy-building, they exemplified the holistic approach of aligning their efforts with the principles represented by each chakra. Their collective endeavor wasn't solely about dispelling falsehoods; it was a profound exploration of truth, resilience, and ethical communication, leaving behind a legacy rooted in integrity and unity.

Our strategies mirrored nature's resilience. We fact-checked like controlled burns, creating barriers of truth to halt the spread of misinformation. Collaborating with experts mirrored the diverse collaboration found in a healthy ecosystem.

In the face of misinformation, we adapted and innovated, initiating programs akin to planting seeds of critical thinking in the community.

Aligning with the 7G Framework and nature's wisdom, we transformed the crisis into an opportunity for truth and enlightenment. Our actions nurtured a more informed and resilient community, echoing nature's principles of resilience and integrity.

I stand here today as Ramji a product of nature's classroom, a messenger of its wisdom. It is my hope that by embracing nature's principles, we can pave the way for Cognos to flourish, to make a positive difference, and to leave a legacy that echoes through the annals of time.

In my journey, triumphs abound, yet perfection remains elusive. Striving for perfection, I edge closer to excellence. Instances arise where principles are inadvertently violated, showcasing the challenges of their implementation.

The emphasis is on me being a perpetual student rather than a master of these principles. They were not invented or discovered by me, but are etched in the very fabric of nature, waiting for those willing to observe, learn, and apply. In essence, they have been organized into a framework, a humble attempt to make sense of the profound wisdom ingrained in our surroundings.

In acknowledging my own imperfections and struggles, I am reminded that I am no different from any of you. We are all navigating the intricate web of these principles, learning, and growing with every step. Thus, the credit for the wisdom embodied in the framework belongs not to me but to the forces of nature that have shaped our world since time immemorial.

With deep humility, I step back from center stage at the inauguration of this groundbreaking event. The true honor rightfully rests upon the shoulders of the unsung heroes in our communication team and every individual who embraced the challenges of this exhilarating journey. Their unyielding commitment propelled the flawless launch of this pioneering initiative, defying formidable odds with unwavering dedication.

To the dedicated members of the Cognos, and especially to our esteemed Department Heads, I extend a heartfelt invitation. Step forward, not merely as individuals but as the embodiment of the collective force that stood firm against the storm. Inaugurate these games, not just as a symbolic gesture but as a profound recognition of your unwavering commitment and resilience. The

Department Heads, representing the workforce's dedication, stand as a testament to our collective strength."

As the team steps forward, the first rays of the sun illuminate Ramji clapping in approval.

The trees stand as silent witnesses to a new chapter unfolding—a chapter where the principles of nature guide not just the individual, but the collective spirit of a dedicated team. The rising sun casting a warm glow on the scene, symbolized a new beginning inspired by the wisdom of the natural world.